THE

SHEFFIELD

BEER + SPIRITS

BIBLE

CW00400531

This book is dedicated to the memory of James Eardley, owner of Brew Foundation, Ecclesall Ale Club and Fulwood Ale Club.

October 1982 to 19 July 2021.

Rest in Peace...

# CONTENTS

06     FOREWORD: JOHN MITCHELL
08     WELCOME
12     BREWERIES & DISTILLERIES
58     PUBS & BARS
96     RETAILERS
122    BEER EVENTS

## ICONIC BREWS

14     ABBEYDALE MOONSHINE
26     FARMERS BELGIAN BLUE
36     SIR ROBIN OF LOCKSLEY
50     JAIPUR
86     O HARA'S SPICED RUM
120    STONES

## INTERVIEWS

10     SEAN CLARKE
70     MIKE POMRANZ
82     JOHN WICKHAM
106    JULES GRAY
118    DEAN HOLLINGWORTH

# FOREWORD
# MITCHELLS WINE MERCHANTS

I am delighted to have been asked to write the foreword for this Sheffield Beer & Spirits Bible. Sheffield is in my blood and our family have now traded at Meadowhead since 1935. Personally, I've been involved in the retailing and wholesaling of beers, wines and spirits for some 54 years with Mitchells. Being from Sheffield makes me very proud of our beer heritage; there are well over 50 breweries in the city region providing around 1,000 different brews each year, meaning we really are spoilt for choice. The many superb pubs, bars and restaurants across our city always serve the finest local beers available, which are forever changing and innovating.

I have always enjoyed a good pint, so back in 2016, when we were seeing the rapid rise in the popularity of craft beer, we decided to build a microbrewery next door to the shop. The brewery is now run by Little Mesters Brewing, who are making some cracking beers (the Original Pale at 4.5% is a must-try!). No wonder we are known as the real ale capital of the world and a popular beer destination, with the likes of Abbeydale, True North, Neepsend, Saint Mars of The Desert and Kelham Island Brewery – just to mention a few! – alongside dozens of craft beer shops on-hand to ensure there's always a pint to satisfy every palate.

In my early days, the brewing trade was dominated by the big five: Bass Charrington, who owned Stones and The Hope & Anchor Brewery; Courage, who acquired John Smiths in 1970 and were taken over by Scottish & Newcastle in 1995, then Heineken in 2008; Allied Breweries, who were a merger of IND Coope, Ansells Brewery and Tetley Walker, but are today known as Carlsberg UK; then Whitbread's at Bridge Street, who bought out Tennents in 1961; and let's not forget local icon Wards on Ecclesall Road!

It wasn't all just about beer; whisky was the staple diet of most middle-class males in the 70s, with massive blended brands such as White Horse, Johnnie Walker, Dewar's, Black & White and Haig. We were the first shop to offer over 100 different malts, remembering back then most distilleries only had one or two expressions, unlike now where some portfolios list 20+ expressions. Today we list over 800+ malts from all over the world.

As it stands, the covid pandemic has changed the way we drink and what we drink. We have seen cocktails at home become a firm favourite, gin is still a steady contender with Sir Robin of Locksley and True North Sheffield Gin leading the local offerings, and whisky is now not only for drinking, but for investing in too. The wine scene has seen customers' palates explode: the love of trying something new, something weird and wonderful, has enabled the underdog grapes to take a turn up front.

I would also like to thank CAMRA for making the real ale scene in Sheffield what it is today. The Campaign for Real Ale was founded in 1971 and is celebrating a 50 year anniversary this year. With what our city has to offer, the folk of Sheffield have never had it so good! So please continue to support the local businesses you'll find celebrated throughout this book. I hope you enjoy the read!

**John Mitchell**
**Owner of Mitchells Wines Merchants**

As we stand today, the covid pandemic has changed the way we drink and what we drink. The wine scene has seen customers palates explode: the love of trying something new, something weird and something wonderful.

# WELCOME TO THE SHEFFIELD BEER AND SPIRITS BIBLE

Sheffield is a city of makers. Innovation and creativity courses through this land like the River Don itself. You can trace this culture of creating back to the 'little mesters' of yesteryear, self-employed craftspeople who, working alone or in small groups, would earn a living making state of the art cutlery and tools in workshops dotted throughout the city. Those days are gone now, but the makers' spirit has remained and can be seen clearly across a range of sectors: art, music, food, events, theatre, digital, manufacturing, to name but a few.

However, there aren't many industries which reflect the city's knack for artisan flair quite as well as its brewing scene. At last count, there are 26 functioning breweries within the city boundaries, from longstanding favourites such as Abbeydale, Bradfield and Kelham Island to exciting newcomers like Heist, Little Mesters and Saint Mars of the Desert. Over the last decade we've also seen a number of small craft distilleries make their name in the Steel City, and there's now even a txotx-style cidery operating out of Shalesmoor!

Working in tandem with these producers is a truly enviable selection of traditional pubs, modern bars, tap houses, public events, specialist beer shops and more, all of which makes for a diverse, thriving drinks scene that Sheffielders can be truly proud of. The Sheffield Beer and Spirits Bible is your handy guide to this industrious community; it's an ode to the people, places and businesses who make this city a vibrant destination on the nationwide beer map. We hope you enjoy reading this book and continue to support local whenever you can. Together we can turn a fine heritage into something truly special for the future.

**Joe Food**
**Exposed Magazine Editor**

# A SPECIAL BREW

*Sean Clarke is co-owner of Beer Central, Sheffield's much-loved beer shop stocking the best of local and worldwide brews. An enthusiastic member of the local beer community, Sean talks us through what makes the Sheffield brewing scene stand out from the rest...*

**After setting up Beer Central in 2013, we quickly found ourselves welcomed into the scene here with open arms.**

The old cliché about Sheffield being the biggest village in the world certainly holds true when it comes to beer. I do think that as a non-Sheffielder I'm able to be quite neutral and honest in assessing things, and I would say that, if anything, people here don't shout enough about how brilliant the city is, especially when it comes to beer. However, that is beginning to change, which you will hopefully see by reading this book, with many people and businesses showing plenty of confidence and really starting to showcase how what we've got here is quite special and unique.

I think one of the great things about brewing in Sheffield is how it caters to all types of drinkers. From Bradfield Brewery's Farmers Blonde to a Belgian Tripel from St Mars of The Desert, the city's beer scene has the ability to tick all the boxes for different types of drinkers. Excitingly, the scene is still growing and there have been plenty of new breweries popping up recently. For example, the likes of Crosspool Alemakers seemed to spring up out of nowhere, so it keeps things fresh and exciting. The established breweries don't rest on their laurels either, and it makes for some great brews all year round. The city's history is an important aspect of its current brewing stature, too. It has a great heritage with big names like Wards and Stones that echo down through the years. Crucially, the place as a whole is very good at showing pride in the past while also moving forward; it's a thriving modern city with two big universities and plenty of smart, forward-thinking people, but it still has that respect for tradition and history. That culture is reflected well in the beer scene, where you have unapologetically traditional breweries doing their thing alongside a range of modern, more craft-inspired outfits. You've also got other local favourites – Thornbridge being a particularly good example – who are very adept at offering a mix of modern classics like Jaipur alongside a range of fresh and exciting craft beer releases.

Another important point is Sheffield's status as the UK's leading outdoor city; this really does lend itself to the traditional cask beers. If you've just finished a beautiful walk in the Peak District, for example, you're probably going to be looking for something easy and refreshing like a pint of Abbdeydale Moonshine – preferably in a country pub with an outdoor bench and a gorgeous view. That experience is something that appeals to all age ranges here, and it lends itself to people being able to adapt to different styles; there tends to be an appreciation for the whole spectrum of beer types – and that's a relatively rare thing for a big city. There's also no shortage of good traditional pubs and smart, modern bars in the city centre who want to sell good beer. The rapidly expanding Kelham Island quarter is a great area for beer; it's another place that highlights the city's industrial roots and is a perfect destination to drink great beers in iconic pubs like The Fat Cat and The Kelham Island Tavern. We're all very lucky to be here, Sheffield is ace!

# BREWERIES & DISTILLERIES

# ABBEYDALE MOONSHINE (4.3%)

**One of the city's favourite easy-supping ales, Moonshine was the first beer worked on by Abbeydale Brewery owner Patrick Morton all the way back in 1996.**

After coming up with the recipe for the popular 5.2% Pale Rider while working at Kelham Island Brewery, Pat was inspired to reproduce the pale, hoppy flavour profile at a slightly more sessionable 4.3% abv.

Light on bitterness, hopped with Willamette, Delta, Citra, Chinook and Centennial, for over 20 years this balanced pale has remained the brewery's most popular beer. It's an accolade nicely supplemented by a whole host of prestigious awards and honours including a bronze medal for Golden Ale at the Champion Beer of Britain Awards 2018, Champion Beer of Yorkshire 2012 and runner-up Champion Beer of Yorkshire 2017 – not to mention being named in 2019 as the most popular cask found on bars around the city over the last decade by Sheffield CAMRA's beer census.

In 2020, the Covid crisis accelerated plans to launch their flagship beer in cans, and by May that year the brewery brought out Moonshine in small pack form allowing their supporters to enjoy their most popular beer from the comfort of home.

**abbeydalebrewery.co.uk**

picture: Mark Newton

# ABBEYDALE BREWERY

8 Aizlewood Rd, Sheffield S8 0YX

@abbeydalebeers

Established in 1996, Abbeydale Brewery have been brewing in Sheffield for 25 years, making them one of the city's most widely recognised breweries who have played an important role in giving Sheffield the reputation for being not only Britain's beer capital, but perhaps the real ale capital of the world.

Famous for their flagship beer Moonshine, pints of which are regularly consumed in pubs across the city, Abbeydale Brewery have grown their offering in recent years, adding to their cornerstone heritage line of hoppy pale ales with modern beer styles such as the popular Heathen IPA, crisp lager Heresy and even a 9.4% Russian Imperial Stout Methulesah, amongst many others in the exciting 'Brewer's Emporium' range.

It is obvious just how passionate the team at Abbeydale Brewery are about beer, and they adore being part of the thriving industry in Sheffield. The Brewery took ownership of popular Fulwood Road pub The Rising Sun in 2005. Managed by Ryan and Nicole Tissington with Head Chef Liam Scott, it has built a reputation in the community for welcoming everyone from all walks of life with their real ale, great food and warm atmosphere.

As one of the city's most beloved – and busiest – breweries knocking out 220 brewer's barrels of up to 15 different beers per week, they put their success down to top-quality, carefully sourced ingredients, a dash of good humour and a love of experimentation in brewing. Here's to another quarter of a century of exciting supping!

# BRADFIELD BREWERY

Watt House Farm, High Bradfield, Sheffield S6 6LG

@bradfieldbrewery

Bradfield Brewery is based on a busy working farm in the picturesque village of Bradfield, situated on the outskirts of Sheffield. Since brewing its first cask ale in 2005, the brewery has grown from strength to the strength with its celebrated Farmers Ale range now available in outlets nationwide.

Using the finest malts, traditional hops and natural spring water from their own borehole, the brewery produce a range of distinctive and award-winning cask conditioned real ales – none more so popular than their famous 'Belgian Blue', a 4.9% winter ale reserved for the festive season whose arrival on pumps in the city's pubs and bars often heralds the official beginning of Christmas celebrations.

Bradfield's online store is a popular destination for anyone looking to experience old favourites and new offerings, with many beers available in bottles, cask and 5L mini-keg form. But if you want the whole experience, you're best off trying one of their sups in a lovely traditional boozer – and luckily they've got three of their own for you to visit: Nags Head Inn, Loxley; King and Miller, Deepcar; and latest addition The Wharncliffe Arms. Expect to find their core ethos of strong community, traditional brewing methods and quality beer represented soundly in each venue.

# BREW FOUNDATION

c/o: Wincle Beer Company, Toll Barn, Wincle, SK11 0QE
@Brewfoundation

When it comes to beer, the father and son team behind independent brewery The Brew Foundation always admitted to being just a little bit obsessed.

For James Eardley and his dad Robert, the idea of brewing their own beer first came to life in a conversation at the local watering hole. They wanted to create "the most drinkable beers on the planet", and after many years of research, what started out as an idea suddenly became a reality when they were offered the chance to brew out of one of Cheshire's famous breweries, Wincle Beer Company. Known as "cuckoo brewing", it gave them the opportunity to benefit from Wincle's experience of craft brewing, while having the freedom to pursue their own adventure.

The main aim of The Brew Foundation is simple – to make beers the Eardleys like to drink themselves. With a series of eight craft beers, from citrus pale ales to extremely drinkable IPAs, there's something to be found for everyone. The beers can be found at The Brew Foundation's two Ale Clubs based in Sheffield, and are also sold at a range of pubs across the city. You'll be sure not to forget them with memorable names such as Hops and Dreams, Little Bitter That and Apollo Thirsteen.

The first beer they developed, First Light, is an American pale ale, which is clean and crisp with a delicate hoppy citrus flavour. Second came Bitter That, which is a fruity, malty bitter that is light enough for summer drinking and comforting enough for winter. It also has a sibling brew, Little Bitter That, which at 3.8% is the session-strength copper-coloured ale they couldn't resist creating.

Apollo Thirsteen also sports a fruity base – grapefruit with Munich and wheat malts with a big dose of Ekuanot added in the fermenting process to add a tropical twist. Customers can choose from a fined and clear cask or a vegan friendly, unfined and hazy cask, showcasing the plethora of options Brew Foundation features.

Targically, aged just 39, James passed away in July 2021. His father and wife Sam have carried on running the brewery and two pubs alongside the Brew Foundation team led by pub manager Georgina Clarke, who can be found at farmers' markets across the city bringing drinkability to the masses and making sure The Brew Foundation is becoming a familiar brand across the North. Look out for their beers at pubs and shops throughout Cheshire, Sheffield, Stoke-on-Trent, Manchester and Wakefield.

# THE BREWERY OF SAINT MARS OF THE DESERT

The Brewery, 90 Stevenson Rd, Sheffield S9 3XG
**@beerofsmod**

**One of Sheffield's newest breweries is The Brewery of Saint Mars of the Desert (or SMOD), located in the industrial Attercliffe neighbourhood of the city and fittingly overlooked by a historic steel foundry.**

Since opening in 2018, owners Dann and Martha have seen their brewery establish a reputation as one to watch on the national craft beer scene, with an innovative selection of hoppy pale ales, Belgian-influenced saisons and barrel/foeder fermented brews in 440ml cans receiving rave reviews all around the country. The results have been of such an impressive standard that, in 2020, it was named one of the ten best new breweries in the world (yes – the world!), not to mention winning the coveted local title of best beer in South Yorkshire by Ratebeer.com in both 2019 and 2020.

Fortunately, not all of SMOD's beer is destined for cans. Their urban-funky taproom welcomes guests to their brewery space, effortlessly blending cool social vibes with a cosy, friendly atmosphere. Here they serve thirds, halves and pints of their much-loved beers with seating available both inside and out. The brewery staff pour as many as nine of their house-brewed offerings, with a limited selection of soft drinks also available. Since the taproom is primarily a space to showcase and celebrate fresh beer, there is no kitchen on-site; however, there are often food vendors and food trucks serving in the courtyard during opening hours. Dann, who has 30 years of experience working with craft beer, explained a bit more about the ethos behind SMOD: "We're a small, family-run artisanal brewery who like to remain very indie-focused in what we do; our beers can be bought at independent retailers in Sheffield and throughout the country. Our small taproom – currently open Fridays and Saturdays – is popular with beer-lovers in the city and gives them the chance to try our brews fresh from the taps."

Next to the taproom you'll find the brewing operation itself housing what we believe is Yorkshire's only koelschip, a large bath-like vessel used for getting extra character out of hops. As such, they've kicked out some truly cosmic brews over the last couple of years – from rich and juicy IPAs such to tart cherry fruit beers. After creating some of the most inspiring brews to come out of the city in the last couple of years, who knows what they'll come up with next!

**For more information on the brewery and taproom opening times, please consult the website at www. beerofsmod.co.uk.**

# CROSSPOOL ALE MAKERS SOCIETY

442 Manchester Rd, Sheffield S10 5DR
@mark.alemakers

*Paying tribute to Sheffield history through a beer range inspired by local events, landmarks and figures, this exciting nano brewery tests out recipes on a small-batch kit situated in the heart of S10, before going on to 'cuckoo brew' their larger batches at breweries around the city and wider Yorkshire area.*

Founder Mark Booth first started brewing from home with a friend, Joe, who'd returned from London to Sheffield. Looking for something different to do other than going to the pub all the time, they decided to take a more hands-on approach to beer sampling, starting up their own small-scale commercial brewing operation, Hopscotch Brewery, from Mark's kitchen in Crosspool.

After getting plenty of positive feedback and a few pubs stocking the Hopscotch beers, Mark decided to take things up a notch and start work on his own brewery. Moving away from the confines of the kitchen, operations were shifted to a garage containing 800L tanks, which then became the spiritual home of Crosspool Ale Makers.

The brewery launched at Cutlery Works' Boozehound bar in February 2019, and Mark began increasing their offering by producing new beers at a range of breweries across the city. "I enjoy the cuckoo brewing aspect, as it keeps me flexible," he says. "I've got a small kit at the original brewery space in Crosspool, so I can use that for testing and expanding the cask range, then the larger breweries I'll go to for brewing the popular beers. My partner Steph helps me test the beers. I might do the brewing, but she's the boss!"

Speaking of popular beers, their biggest hit to date has to be 'Straight Outta Crosspool' – a 5.6% West Coast IPA. The distinctive artwork, designed by Sheffield-based company Lucky Dog, pays homage to hip-hop royalty NWA and looked so impressive it persuaded Mark to return to the original batch and tweak it further to ensure the best brew possible, balancing off the hops to create a flavoursome, malty beer with a classic bitter finish.

Shifting focus from the West Coast of LA to the west side of Sheffield, much of the Ale Makers' range is inspired by local culture and legend. Their first beer, 'Horatio Bright', was named after an eccentric steel merchant who lived on the same grounds as the brewery at the end of the 19th century; New World IPA 'On The Loose' was inspired by the time a herd of cows broke out onto the streets of Crosspool, taking up residence in gardens and shutting off a few roads in the process; while on a more personal note, 'He Ain't Heavy' is dedicated to Mark's brother, who's not a fan of ales but was very much in the market for a decent gluten-free lager.

"That local angle is important to us," Mark explains. "I like to put thought into the beer, but also the story behind it. Naturally, we get a lot of support in Crosspool, but we're getting orders all around Sheffield now. Moving forward, we're looking to get more permanent lines in venues, rotating the cask range and basically getting more of our beer across the city and into the pubs and bars."

# EMMANUALES

Cromwell Street, Walkley, Sheffield, S6 3RN

@emmanuales

**Blessing us with beers of biblical proportions since 2014 A.D, Emmanuales is a craft brewery proudly situated in the heart of God's own county. Following a short sabbatical back in 2018, founder Nick Law has resurrected the brand and re-committed himself to spreading the Good News one well-brewed beer at a time.**

It's not as novel of an approach as it may seem: brewing and religion have gone hand in hand for centuries now. It's an affiliation that can be traced all the way back to the Benedictine monks of the 6th Century, who would offer beer to show hospitality to passing travellers and pilgrims, right through to the modern-day Trappist breweries responsible for some of the best brews on the market.

Nick's foray into brewing began around the backend of 2013, while he was still working at a church in Sheffield. "It was a time when I was questioning a lot of things in my life," he recalls. "I'd always had an interest in beer, but I remember a particular moment when I worked as an estate agent and visited a beautiful house in Nether Edge. It had a hop vine outside, and I remember picking a few hops off this vine and

thinking to myself, 'I could brew some beer with this'. So, I did what any self-respecting millennial would do: started teaching myself how to make beer using YouTube."

The beginning of Nick's beer-making journey coincided with plenty of reflection about his role within the church and the paradigm of his faith. He found that conversations with others were far easier when approaching them from his role as a brewer than as a church worker. "It's a great way to bring people together for discussion, literally putting my own label on it as Emmanuales, which is a blend of 'God is with us' and 'ale'. But we're not about forcing religion down people's throats: just beer!"

With plenty of positive feedback on early efforts and an initial goal to brew a beer as good as Thornbridge's Jaipur, Nick applied for and received his producer's licence in 2015. An opportunity arose to work with The Sheffield Brewery Company, where he eventually became Head Brewer, going on to pick up invaluable experience making award-winning beers and using the house kit to continue brewing for Emmanuales.

Eventually, however, the toll of trying to balance two brands at the same time became too difficult. Despite some huge success for Emmanuales, which included going on Songs of Praise to discuss the brewery, a number of factors combined to convince him to take a step back from brewing.

After setting up Hop Forward, a beer branding and marketing agency, and harvesting a wealth of new contacts and information through travelling the country with his beer podcast, Nick felt inspired to step back into the breach and relaunch Emmanuales, announcing its return with a packed-out event at the Industry Tap. Despite lockdown eventually coming along to spoil the fun, it allowed him space to reflect on the best way to move the operation forward.

After plenty of soul-searching, he has made his decision. "I've taken it right back to the start, with a 100L kit and canning machine kitted out in my cellar, relaunching with a new logo and doing small-batch brews. It's first and foremost about making good beer and having a good time, but if people want to have chat, then let's do that. Emmanuales is a way I can try to express who I am, and I suppose I'm trying to be a bit of a modern monk in terms of offering that hospitality and space to talk to others – along with hopefully very good beer."

# FARMERS
# BELGIAN BLUE (4.9%)

**Nothing says Christmas like a freshly poured pint of Belgian Blue, Bradfield Brewery's beloved winter ale traditionally reserved for the festive season.**

The 4.9% ABV ale is known for its rich, malty flavour, Christmas berry overtones and a slight blue tint – making it a distinctive and popular winter warmer for Sheffielders. The beer was first brewed in 2005 and has since gone on to achieve iconic status in the city; it's widely regarded as a sign that the holidays are coming when bars and beer shops get their first delivery in.

Such is the popularity of Belgian Blue, an average festive period will see roughly half a million pints of the stuff supped by Sheffielders – the very first of which tends to be pulled at one of their brewery taps by owner John Gill to a packed out audience. While many pints are sunk in pubs, equally popular are the cask and 5L mini-kegs available on brewery's website. They have been known to sell out, so ensure you get in early to avoid disappointment!

**bradfieldbrewery.com**

# KELHAM ISLAND BREWERY

23 Alma St, Sheffield S3 8SA

@kelham_island_brewery

**When it opened in 1990, Kelham Island Brewery became the first brewery to launch in Sheffield for over 100 years, starting a wave that carries on to this day.**

With a real drive for cask ale flourishing in the 1980s, Dave Wickett - former owner of The Fat Cat public house at Kelham Island - wanted to jump on the trend.

In 1990 he decided to try his hand at brewing and set up a small kit in the back garden of The Fat Cat. "A pioneer", Ed Wickett, Dave's son and current pub manager calls him: "He truly believed if someone else could do it, or even if someone else wasn't doing it, then why shouldn't he?" And with a gap in the market, Kelham Island Brewery became the first brewery to open in Sheffield in 100 years. For Fat Cat patrons there was a novelty to having their beverages brewed only yards away. It was that appeal which got the business off the ground and spiralling into success.

One example of said success is Kelham Island Brewery winning the Great British Beer Festival in 2004 for what is now one of their most well-known brews - Pale Rider. For Ed, it was the best accolade the business could win, and for Pale Rider to be picked out of hundreds of beers - well, it's easy to see why that became Kelham Island Brewery's defining moment since opening their doors in 1990. Given its celebrity status, it's also no surprise that Pale Rider is considered Kelham Island Brewery's specialty - a favourite amongst both customers and Ed himself.

"It's what we're best known for," says Ed. "It outstrips everything we sell to pubs six to one." Kelham Island and Pale Rider go hand in hand. The beer is brewed at an ABV of 5.2% with a defining nose of fresh citrus and berry fruits and a smooth, juicy malt character. Its deceptively moreish finish belies its strength, so easy does it with this icon!

# LITTLE CRITTERS
# BREWING COMPANY

Unit 5, Neepsend Industrial Estate, 80 Parkwood Rd, Neepsend, Sheffield S3 8AG

@littlecrittersbrewing

*Small in scale but big on quality, the Little Critters microbrewery is based in Neepsend and specialises in brewing award-winning dark beers.*

**Speciality: Stouts**
**Try: Everything!**

"My dad Mark and I started the brewery from scratch in a small shell of a warehouse in Sheffield. We've had several award-winning brewers involved as we've grown and over the years they have trained up one of my best mates, Joe, as Head Brewer. We brew in smaller batches to ensure the beer we get out there is as fresh as possible for consumers. We don't like the idea of sitting on stock."

The Steer family started out as publicans, running well-known pubs such as the Fox & Duck in Broomhill and The Doctor's Orders on Glossop Road. Joe entered the fold as one of their bar staff, and over the years he and Matt accumulated plenty of valuable experience working across a wide range of city centre drinking establishments.

With over a decade of homebrewing under their belts and a couple of popular real ale pubs, they decided in 2014 while making a stout in their kitchen that they would brew mainly for personal use and take bottles into the pubs to test out on regulars. Bit by bit, their confidence grew, and in 2015 the decision was made to step things up by purchasing a small 2,000 sq. ft unit in Neepsend. The following year Little Critters produced its first official brew, a 4.2% blonde session ale called 'Blonde Bear'.

The philosophy behind Little Critters Brewery is just as refreshing as a light ale: unpretentious craft beer made in small batches of 1000L, with an aim to provide something for everyone from their core range. "Fundamentally, we want to make beer that we and other people will enjoy drinking," says Matt. "There's a heavy focus on our dark beers in particular, and we'd like to become known as one of the best makers of craft stouts in the country."

It's an ambition that Matt and the team are well on their way to achieving. A cursory glance at the Untappd app reveals how four of their dark beers – 'Nutty Ambassador', 'King Crow', 'Sultanas of Swing' and 'Coco-nutter' – are all ranked in the top 20 pastry stouts nationwide. Focus is currently directed on their canned range, which did particularly well during lockdown, delivering to suppliers/ wholesalers across the country and direct to customers' doors via their website.

With their cans brought to life in vibrant fashion by Sheffield-born illustrator Jim Connolly, the brewery have developed an instantly recognisable brand, naming their beers with tongue-in-cheek animal-based puns – an idea inspired by their time at the aforementioned Fox & Duck. Matt explains: "We thought it'd be an idea to have the different personalities of each animal reflected in the beer flavours, so notes of Ferrero-Rocher for 'Nutty Ambassador' which features a squirrel on the can, raisins for 'Sultanas of Swing', etc. We don't take ourselves too seriously, we love a cheeky pun and it's important to keep the fun in making and drinking beer!"

**littlecrittersbrewery.com.**

# LITTLE MESTERS BREWING

352 Meadowhead, Sheffield S8 7UJ
@little_mesters_brewing

*The brewery name and logo pay tribute to the 'little mesters', skilled craftspeople who were the backbone of Sheffield's cutlery and toolmaking industries of days gone by.*

Still relatively new kids on the beer block, Little Mesters Brewing are based up at Meadowhead in what was formerly the Mitchells Hop House Brewery. Established in 2020, during the midst of the Covid-19 pandemic, it's safe to say that starting a new business from the ground up was not high on the list of most people's priorities given the economic climate.

However, it was quite the opposite for founders Ben, Simon and Ian. During the pandemic, the trio found themselves with enough reflection time on their hands to realise their long-time ambition of opening a brewery had until then been little more than a dream, so they decided it was time to turn that dream into reality.

The brewery boasts a simple aim – 'to brew great tasting beers that are accessible and enjoyable for everyone' – and if you have tried any of the Little Mesters beers, a highly suppable mix of flavours and styles, you'll have to agree they've already managed to hit their main goal.

The brewery name and logo pay tribute to the 'little mesters', skilled craftspeople who were the backbone of Sheffield's cutlery and toolmaking industries of days gone by. That reputation for high-quality work and production is now mirrored in the brewing of their namesake up at Meadowhead. The logo was brought to life by Sheffield-based designers Oliver Barron (@obarron) and Jack Evans (@jevs.design).

Little Mesters Brewing have already cemented their 'Originals Range' that will be an ever-constant in their offering: a gluten-free 4% traditional lager, 4.5% pale ale hopped with citra, simcoe and cascade, and a 3.9% bitter made using the traditional method of adding golden syrup to the boil. Alongside these, Little Mesters have also released a variety of other beers including a hazy IPA, a trio of limited edition Christmas-themed beers (aptly named the 'Three Wise Mesters') and more recently an easy-drinking 4% blonde beer that has been available on cask across the city.

There have also been some impressive collaborations of note. They have worked with the official supporter's club of the England cricket team the 'Barmy Army', a nationwide brewery collaboration with their interpretation of 'IPA for India' raising money for Sewa UK providing ventilators during the Covid-19 crisis. As well as this, they produced a hugely popular beer and bar snack box with Chef Luke Rhodes, who featured on the 2020 BBC series of MasterChef: The Professionals and worked alongside Maxons of Sheffield, who helped bring to life the 'Yorkshire Mixture' IPA.

Definitely a growing brewery to keep an eye out for and a welcome addition to the city's beer scene – expect much more to come from the Little Mesters team!

The beers from Little Mesters are available to buy on their website (littlemestersbrewing.co.uk) and stocked across the city's bottle shops and bars.

# LOCKSLEY DISTILLING CO.

Portland Works, 20c, Randall St, Sheffield S2 4SJ

**In the beginning of 2013, husband and wife team John Cherry and Cynthia King moved from the US to the UK with a specific goal in mind: to set up a fully-bonded distillery here in the Steel City.**

Sheffield-born John has over 20 years of experience in the booze industry, spending almost half of that time working at a number of salubrious liquor stores in Manhattan. This experience was instrumental for a number of things: building valuable contacts, meeting some inspirational distillers and tasting winning products – all helping to sow the seeds that would eventually bloom into Locksley Distilling Co.

While living in the US, John and Cynthia both witnessed the craft beer scene boom before moving across the pond to sweep the UK around five years later. When craft distilleries began to grow in popularity Stateside, they had an inkling that the same formula would apply. The couple had already planned to return to England for their daughter's schooling, so they decided to put this prediction to the test and began laying groundwork for the launch of their own distilling company.

The family stepped off a plane onto UK soil in the beginning of 2013, and the following day Locksley Distilling Co was registered and flavour development began. Back then you had only a handful of gins on the market – the usual suspects of Beefeater, Gordon's, Tanqueray, Bombay Sapphire and Hendrick's (the latter if you were feeling a little adventurous) – all producers that exclusively made dry gins, so John and Cynthia zoned in on a gap in the market to create Sir Robin of Locksley, the country's first 'sipping gin'.

"We wanted to create something you could drink on its own, a liquid that didn't need a boatload of tonic to counteract the dryness," explains John. "We were looking for something with a similar mouthfeel to a whisky or a bourbon. We had quite a distinctive goal as to where we wanted the gin to be taste and quality-wise; each product we make has to last and have a longevity of at least 20 years."

And so the real hard work began. Using a small distilling pot (or 'still') plotted up in the attic of John's parents' home, the best part of four months was spent on getting the flavour right, coming up with around 104 variations of Sir Robin of Locksley in the process – compelling proof, if needed, of the Locksley ethos that when it comes to distilling, it's a marathon not a sprint.

Of the 104 variants attempted, 79 blends were created using different flavours and strengths. The winning recipe was number 61, which you'll find referenced on the bottle, combining five traditional ingredients (juniper, cassia, angelica, coriander and liquorice) with three contemporary (elderflower, dandelion and pink grapefruit) for the unctuous mouthfeel that moved it away from the dry gin category. It was an instant hit and to this day remains the company's best-selling product.

The process behind their flagship gin is a good analogy for the nature of the business itself: a traditional backbone mixed with a quirky twist or two to stand out from the crowd. The Grade II*-listed Portland Works, their home since 2015, is the perfect base for their operations, steeped in Sheffield manufacturing heritage and housing a community of makers keeping that spirit of innovation alive.

Following the success of Sir Robin of Locksley, and with their prediction of the so-called UK 'ginaissance' coming to fruition, John explains how the company are always looking ahead and diversifying to stay ahead of the competition. "We've taken on more contract work distilling for other brand owners, plus we've collaborated with a number of local companies such as Foundry Coffee Roasters, Thornbridge Brewery and Bullion Chocolate. We do tours and tastings in the distillery, and we'll be picking up the gin schools again this year. Moving forward, we're not limited to gin. It was the starting point, but you'll see over the next 5-10 years all sorts of exciting stuff coming out. There will be more high-quality products with that distinct Locksley angle."

**locksleydistilling.com**

# SIR ROBIN OF LOCKSLEY (40.5%)

**Brought to you by Locksley Distilling Co, their much-loved Sir Robin of Locksley gin made booze history as the UK's first 'sipping gin'.**

Named in homage to folklore legend Robin Hood, said to hail from the Locksley (later to become Loxley) area of Sheffield, the process undertaken to create this game-changing gin involved plenty of patience and experimentation with an array of flavours.

A sipping gin is designed so it can be drunk neat, while also retaining the versatility to work nicely with tonic or in a variety of cocktails. A key element of this is getting the unctuous mouthfeel right, almost similar to what you'd find with a whisky or bourbon, and this sweeter, slightly more viscous result can be achieved by combining three contemporary botanicals of pink grapefruit, elderflower and dandelion with the more traditional elements of juniper, cassia, coriander, angelica and liquorice.

It took the team around eight months to arrive at the perfect recipe, testing over a hundred distillations and blends before coming back to their magical number of sixty-one. It's made using a pot distillation process: eight ingredients go into the pot with a base alcohol, are heated up, turned to vapour, and then quickly turned back into a liquid through a condenser. This traditional technique amplifies all the flavours involved, which are then diluted down and bottled on-site at their distillery based in the historic Portland Works building on Randall Street.

The final tasting notes describe up-front juniper with more delicate aromas of elderflower bubbling through. Deliciously smooth and round on the palate, warm cassia notes are soothed with dandelion. Pink grapefruit adds an underlying sweetness and lingering citrus finish, creating a balanced yet distinctively unique flavour.

**locksleydistilling.com**

# NEEPSEND BREW CO.

Unit 13, 92 Burton Rd, Neepsend, Sheffield S3 8DA
@neepsendbrewco

Perhaps best known for their easy-supping, steady away Neepsend Blonde (4%), this zero airs and graces outfit has been quietly and consistently brewing enjoyable beers since its formation in 2015.

The original brewery was housed next to the River Don, just up from the historic Ball Street Bridge, until in 2020, it moved around the corner to join a host of other independent businesses at 92 Burton Road – not to mention providing delicious fresh tank beer for the Factory Floor bar right on the doorstep of the hugely popular Peddler Market.

Over the past couple of years, the brewery has branched out from their core beers with a broad range of additions, the latest of which include a 4.4% chuckleberry and raspberry hose, 8% cryo hopped DIPA and a 9% tonka, cocoa and vanilla stout.

It's a clear sign that despite its well-established name as one of the Steel City's most reliable breweries, the Neepsend Brew team won't be resting on their laurels and will continue to innovate.

You'll find their fine range of sups at plenty of places across South Yorkshire, including traditional alehouses like The Sheaf View, The Wellington and The Blake Hotel, plus plenty of other reputable establishments and beer shops dotted across the region.

# THE SHEFFIELD BREWERY CO.

Unit 111, JC Albyn Complex, Percy St, Sheffield S3 8BT
@sheffieldbrewery

Since 2006, Sheffield Brewery has operated in the historic Albyn Works, a Victorian red-brick factory space which also houses their charming brewery tap room that opens to the public at weekends.

A longstanding dedication to using world-class malts, hops and yeast strains, mixed with the freshest Sheffield water from the Peaks, has helped the brewery produce an award-winning range of ales, including a flagship core range: Blanco Blonde, Crucible Best, Five Rivers, Get Thi Sen Outdooerz, Seven Hills and the 'darkly delicious' Sheffield Porter and Ruskin Stout.

Their traditional gravity-fed tower brewing system – a real rarity in the UK – has inspired their 'Gravity Brews' selection, which features a range of styles including American IPAs, New Zealand Pales, Baltic Porters, and more.

If you want to try some of their brews on draught, you'll find them down the road at their official tap and real ale hotspot, The Gardeners Rest.

If you're wondering just how they do it, Sheffield Brewery offer popular brewery tours where you can spend a couple of informative hours seeing the process in action, touring the nook and crannies of the historic building, followed by a tutored tasting session with lunch.

# SHEFFIELD DISTILLERY

107-109 Station Rd, Chapeltown, Sheffield S35 2XF

@sheffield.distillery

*The distillery offers a range of products consisting mainly of spirits, like their Assay vodkas, Assay gins and Assay miniatures. These all come in a variety of flavours like strawberry jam and black pepper vodka, rhubarb and custard gin, roasted rhubarb vodka and liquorice gin, as well as the classic flavours.*

**After hosting distillery and tasting nights every couple of weeks (with great success) the next logical step for The Commercial Inn – a specialist real ale and spirits pub located in Chapeltown - was to set up their own distillery.**

Sheffield Distillery was built in the beer garden of the pub, registered as an independent business in 2017, and began distilling in September 2018. With around 400 different types of spirits behind the bar – 130 of which were gins - adding a touch of home to their range seemed like a nice progression for co-founder Paul Harrison and his team.

All the distilling is done using a water-heated copper pot still, their senses and gut instinct… and a little bit of maths. By only using copper equipment they are able to achieve a really clean and syrupy alcohol that is very popular with their customers. Paul likes to make the best quality spirits they can, using whole botanicals as much as possible.

And we think it's safe to say they are well on their way if the awards Sheffield Distillery has won are anything to go by. The business has already racked up six certificates this year from two different international spirits tasting competitions. If that wasn't impressive enough, they've also won two gold medals for their vodka – one in the International Spirits Challenge and the other in the International Wine and Spirits Competition.

The distillery offers a range of products consisting mainly of spirits, like their Assay vodkas, Assay gins and Assay miniatures. These all come in a variety of flavours like strawberry jam and black pepper vodka, rhubarb and custard gin, roasted rhubarb vodka and liquorice gin, as well as the classics.

But it hasn't all been plain sailing, and the business has had to bounce back from a fire which broke out in the distillery in 2020. A blockage in the stills caused pressure to build up and force the top off, spraying out 80°c alcohol. Unfortunately, Paul himself was caught up in the accident and was severely injured. Thankfully, he is on the mend and making a steady recovery. For the business, the fire meant six months of no trading after only being open for two and a half years. But, like Paul, Sheffield Distillery has made its comeback and goes from strength to strength.

# STANCILL BREWERY
Unit 2, Oakham Drive, Sheffield S3 9QX
@stancillbrewery

Born in Barnsley, brewed in Sheffield; the growth of Stancill Brewery since arriving in the Steel City has been a sight to behold. Over eight years, business partners Thomas Gill and Adam Hague have turned a post-uni venture into one of South Yorkshire's largest beer producers, now with two popular venues too: The Albion on London Road and The Closed Shop in Commonside.

Stancill was born when the 150-year-old Oakwell Brewery closed its doors back in 2013, prompting Thomas and Adam – both big fans of Oakwell's trademark Barnsley Bitter – to purchase the brewing and filtration equipment and recreate it themselves. After finding the 'soft water' Sheffield gets from the Peak District to be perfect for brewing, they decided to move the short distance to Parkwood Industrial Estate on Rutland Road, just a stone's throw from the city centre. After

commencing production in 2014, it didn't take long before they were forced to install some new conditioning tanks so they could increase capacity.

Something which made Stancill unique in Sheffield is that they were one of the first local breweries to create a popular craft lager and pilsner – Stancill Lager (4%) and Sheffield Pilsner (5%) – entering an arena that many brewers avoided due to expensive equipment costs. Today the brewery produces around 30,000 pints a week, with an ever-changing range of beers on offer. This now includes an enticing vegan-friendly craft selection featuring ginger pale ale 'Roxie' (4.2%), dry-hopped citrus IPA 'Amazona' (5%) and the punch-packing 'Komrade' IPA (6%), while their core range of classic real ales uphold the traditional brewing methods that the brewery is proud to champion.

# TRIPLE POINT BREWERY
178 Shoreham St, Sheffield City Centre, Sheffield S1 4SQ
@triplepointbrew

A city centre brewery and bar located on Shoreham Street, Triple Point Brewing Ltd is run by father and son duo Mike and George Brook who took on the venue in 2018.

Their award-winning brews are sold straight from tank to glass in a spacious industrial-chic setting, while the taproom also houses Sheffield's famous delightfully dirty burger purveyors, Twisted Burger.

When it comes to brews, Triple Point are impressive all-rounders in the game, catering nicely for lovers of quality lager, IPAs, DIPAs, stouts and porters. Situated a stone's throw from Bramall Lane, their KOP Lager is a natural favourite with Blades fans, while they recently

knocked up a few festive favourites including their Parkin Amber Ale and a baltic porter in a collab with local business Bullion Chocolate. The summer months are well catered for too with 2021 additions to the range including Nekter, a tropically hopped pilsner, and Zatec, a dry-hopped Czech pilsner.

Triple Point boast a spacious outdoor courtyard (something central Sheffield pubs are in need of) which acts as a perfect afternoon suntrap in the brighter months and hosts a variety of social events. However, regulars know that the best seats are inside where you can gaze upon the spectacular brewing kit in all of its exposed glory. Beers with heart made right in the heart of the Steel City – what more could you want?

# STEEL CITY BREWING

Current address: 14A Nutwood Trading Estate, Sheffield S6 1NJ
@Steelcitybrew

*"Another unique element of Steel City Brewing was that they were one of the UK's first cuckoo breweries, which means hiring somebody else's brewery but as a separate company making their own recipes."*

Steel City Brewing was founded in 2009 by Dave Szwejkowski and Gazza Prescott, in response to a lack of hoppy beer in the UK. As unbelievable as that sounds now, back then US-style hopping was still rare here in the UK.

They had both visited America and enjoyed the big hop profiles of the IPAs, but didn't see why hoppy beer needed to always be 6%+ or 'balanced' with sweeter malts. Dave and Gazza then brewed what they referred to as 'Transatlantic Pale Ale', blending a UK-style pale malt 4-5% ABV base with US-style high bitterness (generally 75-120 IBU - International Bitterness Units for the uninitiated) and big late hop and dry hop additions.

Some years later, the US caught onto this idea but called it 'Session IPA', albeit usually less bitter.Another unique element of Steel City Brewing was that they were one of the UK's first cuckoo breweries, which means hiring somebody else's brewery but as a separate company making their own recipes, which has obvious limitations but has allowed the company to set up with minimal capital investment and operate on a part time basis around the owners' full time jobs elsewhere.

Gazza has since left to set up a brewery of his own while Dave still runs Steel City as a cuckoo, now based at Lost Industry Brewing. Some years after Steel City started came the 'craft beer boom' which rendered the original motive redundant, as hoppy beer was everywhere.

The brewery has since taken a more experimental direction, focussing more on adjuncts and barrels than hops, usually in a stout

**Speciality: Stout/Sour**
**Try: Whatever's new**

or sour base. However, as the hoppy beer trend has swung towards sweeter styles like NEIPA, Steel City are looking to give the Transatlantic Pale a comeback!

Names are often inspired by music (metal and goth, plus punk in Gazza's time), or topical mockery (luckily there was an unnamed beer in the tank when Thatcher died, so the long-planned name 'Metal Fatigue' was used).

Starting out almost exclusively cask brewing, Steel City Brewing was an early adopter of keykegs - single-use disposable kegs ideal for export and later, ecokegs. Initially kegging only for export, the brewery later switched to keg for certain styles better suited to it (predominantly sours) and for national distribution via online wholesale. Bottling was started to coincide with local bottle shops opening up, later switching to canning which allowed expansion to nationwide delivery.

Brewing is well known as one of the friendliest and most collaborative industries around, and prior to cuckooing at Lost Industry, Steel City Brewing started off at The Brew Company (now Exit 33) before moving to Little Ale Cart and then the Toolmakers. They have also brewed collaborations with brewers across the UK from as small as Emperor's, a 20 litre(!) brewery rated on Untappd as best in the world, to the twin-160 barrel brew house of Fullers.

As Dave and Gazza both love to travel, they've brewed international collaborations with Marina and Reptilian in Spain, Toccalmatto in Italy, Fantome in Belgium, Freigeist in Germany, and Kocour in the Czech Republic. Steel City also host an annual 'mega-collab' where a dozen breweries and a couple of local pubs get together to play cricket, have a barbecue, drink each other's beer and brew something crazy while they're at it.

# TAPPED BREW CO

Tap Platform, 1b Sheaf St, Sheffield City Centre, Sheffield S1 2BP

@**tappedbrewco**

*Being situated in a restored Edwardian dining room steeped in history at one of the UK's busiest train stations really gives Ben Tysoe (head brewer) and the team a unique environment to brew in.*

Imagine ordering a beer at your local and being able to watch the brewing process from start to finish. At Tapped Brew Co. that's the reality and not just a novel idea. Back in 2009 the term 'craft beer' was far less well known than it is these days, and Jon and his team at Pivovar Group simply wanted to sell their customers the biggest range of the best beer they could offer.

They started off by restoring the former train station refreshment rooms, turning them into Sheffield Tap. Then, after opening a couple more taps across the country, an expansion was needed back in Sheffield, and Jon and his team couldn't resist installing their own microbrewery in the adjacent First Class Refreshment Room. And thus, Tapped Brew Co. was born.

Being situated in a restored Edwardian dining room steeped in history at one of the UK's busiest train stations really gives Ben Tysoe (head brewer) and the team a unique environment to brew in. On brew days the customers are fascinated by seeing the brew process in action. The team offers a meet-the-brewer experience, answering the popular questions like how beer is made, what the smells are, how long it takes from brewing the beer to getting a pint from the bar etc.

– all resulting in a unique experience that you really don't see in many bars.

"You can't get beer much more local than this," Ben says. "The sights and smells of beer being brewed in these opulent surroundings in front of travellers and regulars alike is a big attraction for the Tap."

Tapped Brew Co. strives to achieve well balanced beers by considering not only the hop profile but the malt profile too, ensuring both are spot on. Achieving consistency in the finished product is their main goal. Currently, they're concentrating on lower strength ales; these styles have the highest demand with drinkers of cask beers. The most popular current beer the brewery produces is Sheaf Street Pale – a session IPA named after the location of The Sheffield Tap. Their flagship beer over the years is Mojo, a 3.6% session pale. As it is low strength, it's an ideal beer for those drinkers who like to go in and have a few pints while waiting for their train, or who simply enjoy watching the world go by in a beautiful building.

With all this variety and dedication to giving their customers the best, we can see why Tapped Brew Co. has been awarded 'Best Brew Pub' by Ratebeer.com on numerous occasions, and the beautiful architecture more than accounts for their heritage awards!

Tapped Brew Co. – Traditional cask beer with a nod to the modern drinkers.

# THORNBRIDGE BREWERY

Riverside Brewery, Buxton Rd, Bakewell DE45 1GS
@thornbridge

Thornbridge Brewery's story began in 2005 at Thornbridge Hall, the home of co-founder Jim Harrison. Along with friend and fellow Sheffield Wednesday fan Simon Webster, the pair installed a second hand 10-barrel brew kit within the grounds of the Thornbridge Hall estate.

Hiring two young and passionate brewers, the first beer produced was Lord Marples, a 4% classic bitter which remains a staple within their range to this day. Their next task was to brew something a little different - an IPA that packed a punch in terms of both flavour and ABV – and so, in mid-2005 Jaipur was created.

You probably recognise the name and would be able to spot its distinctive orange branding; it is of course known as Thornbridge's biggest breakthrough. Simon Webster, CEO and co-Founder confirms that "Jaipur is still regularly cited as 'the beer that got me

**Speciality: Japiur - one of the most decorated beers of all time!**

into beer', with drinkers still keen to come and enjoy it at the source in our taproom". The truth is that it remains one of the leading contributors to Thornbridge's widely held regard as one of the pioneers of the craft brewing movement in the UK, as well as picking up both national and international awards to this day. With Jaipur catapulting Thornbridge into the spotlight, demand soon outstripped supply and the need for a new brewery became clear.

They scaled up commercially in 2009, installing a new state of the art brewery at Riverside, Bakewell allowing Thornbridge to not only meet demand but also develop their range of beers. The original Thornbridge Hall kit now sits alongside the taproom at Riverside, allowing their brewers to experiment with new recipes, create bespoke small batch brews and continue to produce quality cask.

Thornbridge consistently have over 40 beers available to purchase directly online in can and bottle, with further beers available in draught format for trade customers. They also offer the 'Thornbridge Experience', which provides a history on all things Thornbridge, an explanation of the brewing process and a tutored tasting of 6 thirds of beer. Located in the beautiful Peak District town of Bakewell, their taproom serves 16 of the freshest Thornbridge beers along with artisan pizzas, both of which are a real draw for locals and tourists alike.

# JAIPUR (5.9%)

**One of the most iconic IPAs in the Sheffield City Region, and indeed, the whole nation.**

With a reputation in the craft beer community for being the catalyst that would begin the rolling out of a whole host of IPAs and Double IPAs, we couldn't do an iconic brews piece and not give Jaipur its own special mention. This beverage is truly considered as one of the most influential beers of the last fifteen years – an icon and a friend, if you will. There are many ways in which Jaipur is a first: for Thornbridge, it was the first beer the business brewed and was ultimately instrumental in placing them on the map; for its drinkers, many have named Jaipur as 'the beer that got me into beer', the start of a journey for thousands up and down the country.

The fortitude of a good IPA (i.e. Jaipur) holds its own beside rich flavours and intense spices. Jaipur itself has a vibrant and colourful tropical fruitiness on both the nose and palate. A dry, crisp biscuitiness before the bitter and fruity finish is also nicely achieved in this beverage. With this in mind, we recommend pairing this classic with a hearty curry, aromatic and bursting with flavour. A green curry is ideal - the lemongrass and coriander will merge well with the citrus and herbal hops. The hops used in Jaipur give it that energetic and zesty fruitiness and despite its 5.9% ABV, it is an easy drinking beer as long as you go steady!

**thornbridgebrewery.co.uk**

# TOOLMAKERS & THE FOREST

6-8 Botsford St, Sheffield S3 9PF // Rutland Street, Sheffield S3 9PA
@toolmakers-brewery

*Toolmakers officially started trading in 2013 and has been creating great brews ever since, including their Lynch Pin dark ale, Razzmatazz blonde and Flounge Noir stout.*

**Speciality: Lynch Pin Dark Ale
Try: Flounge Noir Stout**

**If you've ever found yourself on a night out at the Gardeners Rest or Old Workshop in Neepsend, and fancied trying somewhere new for size, then Toolmakers and their pub, The Forest, are just a two minute walk away.**

A family-run brewery business and venues owned by Olie and Marion, the brewery and its tap room were launched back in 2006 after Olie bumped into the owner of White Rose Brewery in The Commercial pub in Chapeltown. The two men got to chatting about the brewery business and Olie was instantly intrigued.

Under the guidance of his new teacher, he went on to spend the next two or three years learning the trade until the time came for them to buy their own property on Botsford Street. Toolmakers Brewery officially started trading in 2013 and has been creating great brews ever since; including their Lynch Pin dark ale, Razzmatazz blonde and Flounge Noir stout.

The tap room located on site is renowned for offering regular live music and entertainment, including comedy clubs, regular rhythm and blues nights and their Sunday open mic nights, while it's also often used for wedding celebrations these days too.

When it comes to memorable moments, there have been plenty, including their 'Day of Heroes' event they hosted back in April 2018. The 1940s themed day, dedicated to paying tribute to the heroic deeds of WWII, included mannequins of some of the war's most memorable veterans, authentic military vehicles, and even the chance to meet former British paratrooper, veterans' campaigner and author Ben Parkinson MBE. As well as providing a historically immersive experience for their patrons, the day was run in aid of The Pilgrim Bandits charity.

Just around the corner you'll find The Forest, which like Toolmakers Tap Room sells only the brewery's own ales and offers regular live music as well as pool nights and a very decent Sunday lunch.

Marion and Olie are very passionate about keeping their business inclusive and inviting to all. As soon as anyone sets foot over the Toolmakers or Forest threshold they automatically become part of the family - and like good Northerners do, Marion and Olie look after their own. They're both determined to remove the stigma of it being unusual or unheard of for a customer to frequent a brewery or pub, and drink and dine alone - especially single women!

They're all about lending a helping hand; after all, that is how Toolmakers essentially came about. So whether it's the live music, real ale or just a great atmosphere you're going for, these are two venues - right on the doorstep of Kelham Island - you should be quick to check out.

# TRUE NORTH BREW CO.

47 Eldon Street, Sheffield, S1 4GX
**@truenorthbrewco**

**True North Brew Co. is a leading independent pub, bar and restaurant group with 14 venues spread across South Yorkshire and Derbyshire. They have a brewery and distillery based in Sheffield centre producing an excellent range of beers and distilling the famous 'Sheffield Dry Gin' – which upon launch was the first gin to be bottled and distilled in the Steel City for over 100 years.**

The company started with the Forum Café Bar and Halcyon on Devonshire Street, two venues at the forefront of hybrid spots offering chilled-out daytime hangouts which transformed into eclectic late-night bars responsible for many a memorable evening out. Over the years the company has grown at a steady rate, developing its offer and taking many of their customers on the journey with them. Such is the wide-ranging appeal of their venues, you will often get several generations from the same family visiting to enjoy some truly Northern hospitality.

Every True North venue is unique in its offering and design but there are a few similarities that run throughout them all: the staff will be some of the friendliest, knowledgeable, passionate and creative people you'll ever be served by; the food and drink will be excellent quality and perfectly presented; the atmosphere will be spot on, and you won't want to leave. During lockdown, 'True North at Home' was launched with great success as the residents of Sheffield were able to get their pie fix delivered direct to their door. Thankfully, this is a service they have kept on since reopening and with a wide number of venues across the Steel City and beyond there's bound to be one near you.

ALL SHE WANTED WAS
TO BE SOMEONE'S MOST
PRECIOUS PERSON

# SHEFFIELD DRY GIN NAVY STRENGTH (57%)

A Steel City take on a maritime classic, this is our navy strength Sheffield Dry Gin with added rock samphire and sea buckthorn.

**Tasting notes:**
Juniper led with full-bodied, bold flavour and subtly sweet undertones, smooth on the palate.

# GUNPOWDER GIMLET COCKTAIL

Sheffield Dry Gin Navy Strength is best served blended with Franklin & Sons Natural Indian Tonic Water with a squeezed wedge of orange and an orange peel twist. But if you want to turn this full-bodied, bold gin into a fresh cocktail then follow our Gunpowder Gimlet recipe.

**50ml Sheffield Dry Gin Navy Strength**
**12.5ml fresh lime juice**
**12.5ml gomme**
**1 lime wheel**

**1. Pour the liquids into a Boston shaker filled with ice.**
**2. Shake well for 30 seconds.**
**3. Strain using a hawthorne strainer into a chilled coupe glass.**
**4. Garnish with a lime wheel.**

# PUBS & BARS

# ALE CLUB

429 Ecclesall Rd, Sharrow, Sheffield S11 8PG // 4 Brooklands Ave, Fulwood, Sheffield S10 4GA
@aleclubpub // @aleclubful

After dipping their toes in the waters of brewing, The Brew Foundation decided to extend their reach into opening up a series of brewery taps. The Ecclesall Ale Club and its sister venue The Fulwood Ale Club are micro pubs serving a range of cask, keg, bottles and cans from indie breweries across the globe – but the Eardleys always ensure one of their beers is on the bar at all times.

The Ecclesall Ale Club is a cosy micro pub and bottle shop located at 429 Ecclesall Road, Sheffield, and is the Brew Foundation's flagship venue. The club started off with 5 cask lines, 8 keg lines and around 130 bottle/can lines but has highlighted its potential to expand in the future. After a successful couple of years in the venue, the expansion into The Fulwood Ale Club at 4 Brooklands Avenue was met with an overwhelmingly positive reaction. A nano pub rather than a micro pub, it is speculated that it could possibly be the smallest bar in Sheffield – so get there early to get a seat! Located in a former butcher's shop, the former cold room is now in use as a cellar, and meat hooks hang from the ceiling to hark back to the pub's origins. Like its big sister, The Fulwood Ale Club specialises in real ale and craft beer from independent breweries but also operates as a take out bottle shop too.

The Ale Clubs' décor is inspired by old school private members' clubs; meaning lots of dark wood, low level lighting and lots of curios to look at whilst having a pint. As well as a wide range of beers, the Ale Clubs also offer craft gins, whisky, rum, vodka, brandy, wines, prosecco and soft drinks. Classic pub snacks such as pork pies, scotch eggs, pickled eggs, crisps and peanuts can also be found to satisfy the watering hole munchies.

The Ale Clubs' and Brew Foundation's main aim is to stock the beers that their customers want to drink as well as a hub for the community. As a result of this, they accept ideas for beers to stock – providing a way for their customers to get involved and cementing their place as a real heart of the community.

**Speciality: Gluten free APA 'Free Beer' Try: C-Bomb - citrus session IPA**

# THE BEER ENGINE

17 Cemetery Rd, Highfield, Sheffield S11 8FJ
@beerenginesheff

Tucked away on Cemetery Road, just a stone's throw from the ever-bustling London Road and Ecclesall Road runs, it's always worth nipping off the beaten path to visit this hoppy haven that's become of staple of the beer scene since opening its doors in 2015.

True to its name, this cosy watering hole pumps out an ever-changing selection of keg and bottled beers alongside a solid choice of whisky and gins. The decor is based on an old-school boozer with a few modern twists and their hidden gem beer garden out back, adorned with quirky artwork and plants, is a popular destination for thirsty Sheffielders during the warmer months and football fans on matchday due to its close proximity to Bramall Lane.

On the bar you'll find six handpull cask pumps and eight kegs, including regular and guest real ales as well as continental lagers, craft beers and a good selection of local offerings. A tempting small plates menu complements the drinks selection, rotating on a monthly basis with a solid variety of vegetarian and vegan dishes and gluten-free options.

# KELHAM ISLAND TAVERN

62 Russell St, Sheffield S3 8RW
@kelhandislandtavern

A longstanding fixture on Kelham Island's revered real ale circuit, this historic building dates right back to the 1830s when it first operated under the name 'The Sawmaker', later becoming 'The White Hart' before finding its current title during the 90s.

Following a period of closure, the building was saved from dereliction and reopened in 2002 with a commitment to becoming one of the best real ale pubs in the region. The venue has consistently achieved this goal over the preceding two decades, winning an array of awards including Yorkshire Pub of the Year (2004, 2007-2009) and Sheffield CAMRA Pub of the Year (2004-2011, 2014-2018, 2020), growing in stature with the popularity of the Kelham area to become a staple on any beer lover's list.

It's a simple but effective formula that leads to such acclaim: a cosy, welcoming interior complemented by a beautifully well-kept suntrap garden and a revolving selection of 12 cask beers and 4 keg. It's as traditional as they come, with sarnies and pork pies on the bar, Morris dancers and live folk music on weekends. Long may its reign continue!

# BENCH

7b Nether Edge Rd, Nether Edge, Sheffield S7 1RU
**@benchsheffield**

Bench started life as a side project for owners Jack and Ronnie back in 2018, alongside their day jobs at Public, where they were part of the team that won Observer Food Monthly's best place to drink 2018.

They hosted three sold out pop-ups in some of their favourite independent businesses around Sheffield with nights in diverse settings from flower shops to design studios.

The focus of these evenings was communal drinking and dining, with the food centred around open fire cooking, and the drinks closing the divide between bar and kitchen, always sharing and pairing ingredients.

After their huge success as a pop-up, it was the right time to find a more permanent place to call 'home' and their bistro/bar/wine shop 'Bench' opened in October 2020 in the neighbourhood area of Nether Edge, Sheffield.

## BENCH'S NEGRONI

**20ml gin**
**20ml Campari**
**20ml sweet vermouth**
**40ml chilled water**
**5ml orange oil**
**Pinch of salt**

To batch our negroni, scale up the ingredients to the amount you need and pour them all into an empty bottle or any Tupperware you have lying around. Leave to chill in the fridge for a few hours. Once chilled, we pour ours into a frozen coupette.

# BERLIN CALLING, RANMOOR CASTLE BEER AND SPIRITS AND BEER DOG

Berlin Calling, 18-20 Barber Rd, Sheffield S10 1ED // Ranmoor Castle, 392 Fulwood Rd, Sheffield S10 3GD // Beer Dog, 108 Charlotte Rd, Highfield, Sheffield S1 4TL

*"Music is very much in the venue's DNA, and even the name is a reference to Ray's love of DJ Paul Kalkbrenner, and in particular his album Berlin Calling, which is his favourite album."*

**Not previously known for its electronic music scene, in November 2019 a cutting-edge bar sprang up in Commonside offering a heady mix of top techno and lots of lovely German beer!**

Berlin Calling was opened on Barber Road by a couple of friends who share a love of electronic music and Berlin. Already the owners of Street Art Tattoos, Raimonds Dobelnieks (Ray) and Hardijs Deinats branched out into the next-door unit and transformed the former Premier shop into a minimalist bar with a 'Berlin vibe'.

Co-owner Ray explained: "It is Berlin, but it's not meant to be a typical German pub. We only have German beers on tap, because it makes sense, but it's meant to be an electronic music venue, where you can come and chill.

"I've always been into electronic music, and Berlin is the best place in the world to experience it. I go five or six times a year because I love the underground scene and before we opened this place, I spent a week in

Berlin trying all the different places. Our place has definitely got its minimalist Berlin-vibe from those trips.

"Sheffield is quite famous for its underground scene, I'm not in that age group anymore, but still, now and again, I forget about the suffering the next day and go to events at Hope Works, Night Kitchen and Yellow Arch, and new places like Dryad Works. We're a pre-party place for underground events at these kind of places in the city."

Music is very much in the venue's DNA, and even the name is a reference to Ray's love of DJ Paul Kalkbrenner, and in particular his album Berlin Calling, which is his favourite album.

As well as the music though, Berlin Calling also boasts a pool table, foosball table, Xboxes, plenty of space to chill out with friends, and even German snacks. Everything in the bar has been salvaged or reused, and local street artists Affix and Trik09 have created the wall

murals in the bar and toilets.

"I've put my heart into this" says Ray: "I have friends who are builders who helped me realise my childhood dreams, because every boy wants a playground, and I'm going to keep pushing myself to bring more of Berlin to this space. I want this to represent the city and the music."

The venue was a great success and gained a reputation for good beer as well as banging tunes. However, not satisfied with one new venture, nearly a year later Ray and Hardijs set upon a new challenge, to open their own local bottle shop in Ranmoor.

With the help of Dram Shop owners, Tony and Sandra Oakes, the guys opened the new upscale bottle shop in August 2020, specialising in high end beers at affordable prices.

Ray said: "Tony and Sandra are friends of ours and they helped us open our first shop,

guiding us through the processes. They have 40 years' experience and people have trust in them, so it was a big help in the beginning.

"It's different to Berlin Calling. Ranmoor Castle is more like a top of the range beer shop, with spirits you can't buy in supermarkets, a better wine selection than in your local corner shop, and of course, a lot of beer.

"We have local shelves, so local Sheffield breweries, as well as British breweries, then we have Scandinavian shelves and German fridges with over 100 German beers. We have loads of cans and craft beers and plenty of Belgian beers.

"As our alcohol sales experience grew, we became more comfortable and wanted to open more shops. The businesses, to me, are all in line with each other, so we had the tattoo shop, then we opened Berling Calling, then Ranmoor Castle."

On a roll, the owners of the Barber Road bar and Ranmoor shop teamed up with Crosspool Ale Makers to create a new premium craft ale bottle shop and tap room on Charlotte Road, on the doorstep of Bramall Lane stadium.

The Beer Dog, which opened in June 2021, features four cask lines courtesy of the West Sheffield brewery, the first time the Crospool-based beer makers have had their own permanent taps anywhere. The beer shop also boasts a varied range of cans and bottles from all over the world with a special emphasis on unusual German beers.

Ray boasted: "We have the largest German beer selection within at least 100 miles. In Berlin Calling and Ranmoor we have beers you can't get anywhere else because we have

one supplier who brings the craziest German beer ever, and we have even more of that at Beer Dog.

"This is not somewhere to come and get cheap beer, it's about quality and choice. We're not just an off-licence. Mark, from Crosspool Ale Makers, supplied us with loads of beer in Ranmoor, so we chatted with him about installing some beer lines here, and now we have four of his beers on tap."

Mark Booth (Crosspool Ale Makers) added: "It's exciting for me because it's the first time I've ever had permanent lines in a bar. Don't get me wrong, I might swap beer with people who bring beer from other places and if it's cool enough I'll bring it in. But, to start with, it'll be my beers on tap. It's a big step for the brewery.

"It's great to get on board with these guys because you've seen Berlin Calling, and how cool it is. They've got beer from all over. It's not just about having German beers, it's about having something for everyone.

"Some of the stuff in here, I wouldn't be able to get anywhere else, especially on this side of the ground, where, other than the city centre, you haven't got a great deal going on in the immediate area around the football ground."

They are hoping that Beer Dog will be the catalyst for regeneration in the area. "This place needs something extra." says Ray, "If you look around, there's loads of cool people walking around, but there's nothing around unless you go into the city centre. We want to be a cool beer shop with a large selection of beers that serves this side of town.

"Beer, football, and hot dogs, what can go wrong?"

# MIKE POMRANZ

# HOW D'YA LIKE
# THEM APPLES?

As the book's title suggests, this is predominantly a guide to the beer and spirits on offer in Sheffield, but it would be remiss of us not to at least talk about cider for a page or two, given that Sheffield now boasts its very first cidery and cider brand.

That's right, it turns out you don't have to look as far as Herefordshire or Somerset to find great cider anymore; we have a certified cider professional right here in Sheffield and he has big plans to make Steel City apples even more interesting.

Although not a Yorkshireman by birth, having moved here from the States five years ago, we're claiming Mike Pomranz and his all-new cider brand Exemption Ciderhouse as one of our own.

Fermenting cider (note, not brewing – we're not talking beer here) has been a passion of Mike's for several years but he hasn't always been quite such an avid advocate. Beer has always been his main love, and his first visit to a cider festival only came about when he was asked to cover it for Food and Wine magazine, as part of his day job as a freelance writer.

"All the different ciders blew my mind." Mike explains, "There is obviously just bog-standard stuff you can get everywhere but when you get to the true, good cider it can be super complex and funky. It can have wine-like complexity. I've had ciders that tasted closer to a Riesling than some Rieslings."

From this maiden voyage of discovery into a sea of cider, Mike set out on a course to learn more about the process of cider making, which led on to him to become a certified cider professional with the American Cider Association, a journey that recently culminated with him realising his dream of starting his very own cidery, right here in Sheffield.

Once Mike realised that all he needed to begin producing his own cider was to find some wild apples, stick them in the boot of his car, take them home and ferment them, he never looked back, making his first batch with apples he had literally found under an apple tree by the side of the road, in 2014.

"It was really, really nice," says Mike, "and that just opened my eyes. I realised it isn't that tricky; you can just use random apples and try to coax whatever fruit flavours or interesting qualities out of them.

"That's kind of been my philosophy all the way through to this current project. When we moved here, I noticed that a lot of people have apple trees, and a friend didn't want their apples, so I made cider out of them and it was incredible."

So good in fact, that he saved the yeast and that has now become his house yeast strain, which he used in the four-month fermentation stage of his first bottled batch of Exemption Ciderhouse cider, pleasingly titled Wild Tarts Can't Be Broken, in reference to the drink's sour notes.

> **GOOD CIDER CAN BE SUPER COMPLEX AND FUNKY. IT CAN HAVE WINE-LIKE COMPLEXITY. I'VE HAD CIDERS THAT TASTED CLOSER TO A RIESLING THAN SOME RIESLINGS.**

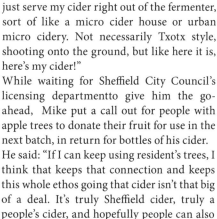

The small run of just 40 bottles went on sale earlier this year, receiving rave reviews from those lucky enough to get their hands on the limited batch. Following this test run, the next stage for Mike and Exeption Ciderhouse, which takes its name from a quirky British exemption that allows anyone to brew up to 7,000 litres of cider without paying duty, is to turn his hobby into a fully-fledged business, with plans for a 1000 litre batch for next year, as well as the even more exciting prospect of a Basque-style Txotx cider house called The Cider Hole, in Shalesmoor's shipping container development, Krynkl.

Mike said: "You go to these cider houses in the Basque country, and you walk into these rooms, which are full of giant barrel fermenters and they call 'Txotx!' and open the tap and the cider shoots out. I was thinking that it would be awesome and pretty exciting to just serve my cider right out of the fermenter, sort of like a micro cider house or urban micro cidery. Not necessarily Txotx style, shooting onto the ground, but like here it is, here's my cider!"

While waiting for Sheffield City Council's licensing departmentto give him the go-ahead, Mike put a call out for people with apple trees to donate their fruit for use in the next batch, in return for bottles of his cider.

He said: "If I can keep using resident's trees, I think that keeps that connection and keeps this whole ethos going that cider isn't that big of a deal. It's truly Sheffield cider, truly a people's cider, and hopefully people can also become a little more educated in something that people in this country mostly take for granted."

# CUBANA

Unit 4 Leopold St, Sheffield City Centre, Sheffield S1 2JG

@cubanatapasbar

For the past 20 years Cubana has been a hot staple in Sheffield, with its Latin music, salsa dancing, tasty tapas food and Havana- style cocktails infusing a vibrant explosion of joy into a rainy English day. Bringing colour to the city, Cubana is perfect for drinking and dining in a fun-filled environment. Inside you'll find a spacious bar filled with a variety of food, drink and music from around the world in the only cultural hub of its type in Sheffield.

Co-owner Adrian Bagnoli first discovered his passion for Latin music whilst visiting a Brazilian nightclub called the Maracanã in Florence, Italy. Falling in love with the lively atmosphere, he came to realise that this was what Sheffield needed. He started by launching Sheffield's first Latin club night, "Viva Salsa", in 1995 at city centre night spot Club Uropa. In 2000 Adrian joined forces with Brad Charlesworth to open Cubana Tapas bar on Trippet Lane, where they were met with huge success before unleashing Cubana onto Leopold Square in 2014.

The eclectic atmosphere carries through into the culinary experience. Their extensive menu has won national acclaim, combining classic Spanish tapas with South American flair and flavour, which includes both meat and plant-based options. Accompanying the tasty tapas is an award-winning rum collection, quality wine list and a plethora of exotic cocktails, promising to add a liveliness and sparkle to your evening out. With one of the widest ranges of rums in the city, from both the local area and the wider international stage, there's something to suit even the pickiest of tastes. From Agricole rums from Martinique and Haiti, to Demerara rums based in Cuba itself, the plethora of options span many continents and cultures.

When you think of Cubana you immediately think of live music; there are regular performances from local and nationally renowned musicians almost every night. They also regularly host dance classes including Cuban salsa, Argentine tango and bachata from the Dominican Republic. With this in mind, Cubana organises one of the biggest outdoor salsa events in the country: 'Salsa In The Square', which takes place over three bank holiday Sundays each year and attracts hundreds of people for a mix of live Latin music, salsa displays, dancing and more. The event has become a cornerstone of Sheffield's cultural calendar.

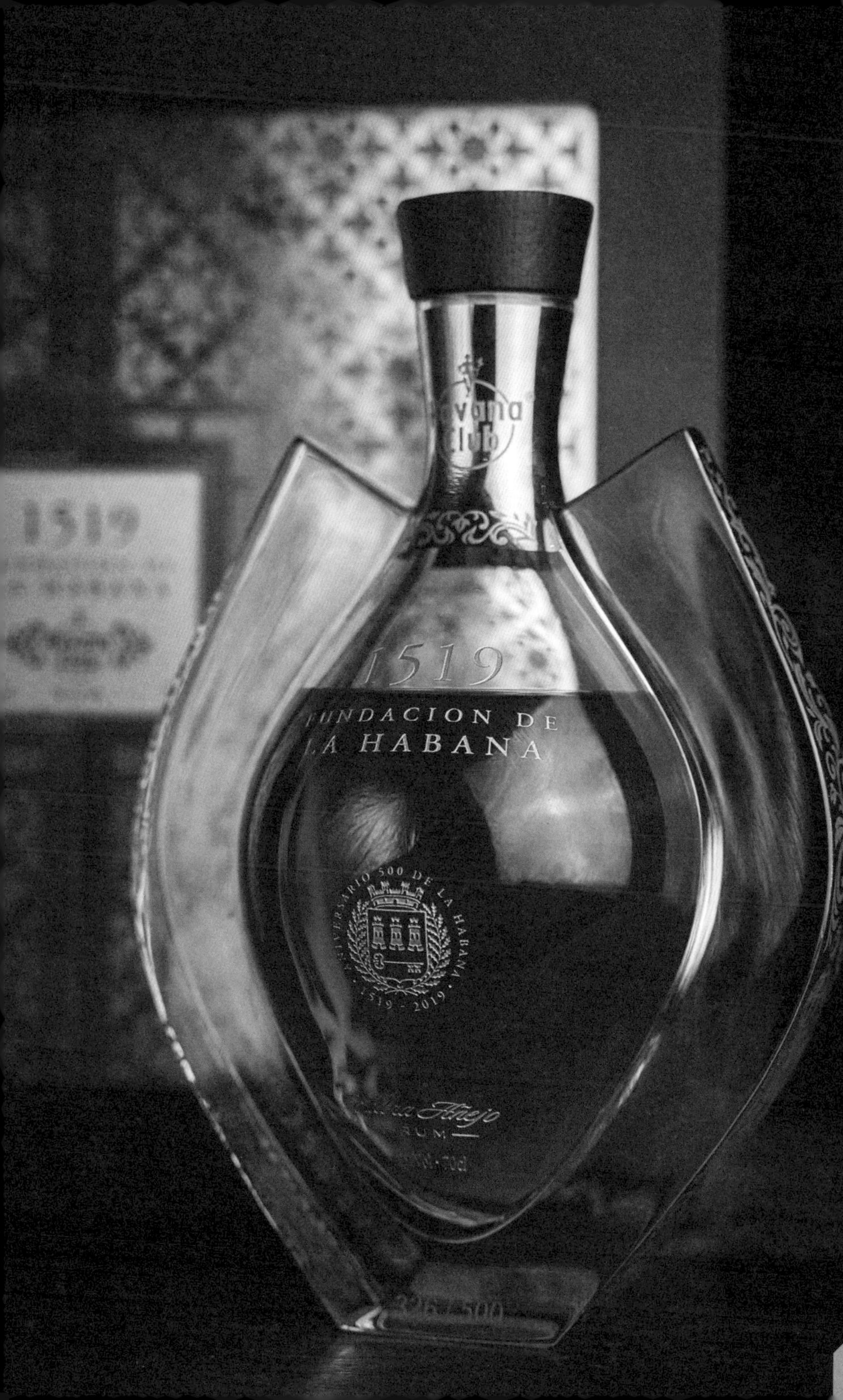
1519
1519 - 2019

# DEAD DONKEY

240 Abbeydale Rd, Nether Edge, Sheffield S7 1FL

@**deaddonkeybar**

*Well known to any frequent visitors to the Broadfield pub on Abbeydale Road, brothers Ed and Doug Daly left for pastures new in 2018, opening their Dead Donkey bar just yards down the road.*

Originally looking at places in Crookes and Kelham Island, the Daly brothers were never really sold by any of the buildings they'd looked at but when the rumours were confirmed that Mr Pickles' Food Emporium at 240 Abbeydale Road wasn't going to be reopening, they set their sights on the venue which is literally yards away from Ed's house.

"It was completely accidental, finding this place," Ed explains. "We found it online but it turned out it was being let by the husband of our mum's colleague. Doug lives just off Chesterfield Road and we've spent most of our lives here."

Being so closely tied to the area, the brothers in beers know exactly what works for their clientele and a huge part of their success since opening has been their accessibility. Regardless of your inclination, whether it's craft beer, wine or cocktails, their knowledge of booze and reasonable pricing will likely be a unique part of the experience.

"We've got beers from here, there and everywhere, basically. "We've also got a big whisky selection too, because that's our other vice. If we're at Starmore Boss then it would be rude not to pick up, say, 50 bottles of whisky, wouldn't it?"

"The wines are also supplied by Starmore Boss so you know that there's no cheap plonk on the menu, but we want to price them as reasonably as possible to be alongside other venues in the area but ensuring it's top notch liquid in the bottles!"

The egalitarian nature of the business comes from years of working in hospitality. They'd always wanted to open a bar together and are passionate about what they do, but are also very aware of the pitfalls, which has given them a very clear vision of what they want from their bar.

"There's no un-diplomatic way of saying this, but the catering industry is just crap," says Ed. "You work unsocial hours, you can't make plans with friends or family, you're on minimum wage and we've been on the receiving end of that for years."

"We're paying our staff the Living Wage," adds younger brother Doug. "We're closing 11pm-ish and closed Mondays which enables us to give the team a four day week and help them maintain a healthy work/life balance."

# THE FAT CAT

23 Alma Street, Sheffield S3 8SA

@fatcatsheffield

**A centrepiece of the Steel City's real ale scene since the early 80s, The Fat Cat is still very much the jewel in Kelham Island's after hours crown.**

Fed up with frequenting pubs and being surrounded by cigarette smoke and blaring music, too loud to hold a coherent conversation with his pals, Dave Wickett decided enough was enough.

He dreamed of spending his Friday nights in a relaxing pub where he could enjoy uninterrupted conversation over a good beer. So, in 1981 he bought The Fat Cat and transformed it into the first pub in Sheffield to promote a smoke-free environment for real ale and homemade food.

The business had its fair share of struggles; from a less than ideal location in a heavily industrialised area with minimal foot traffic to many turning their noses up at this new venture, finding it laughable. If only those doubters knew how times would change. Now, The Fat Cat is recognised nationally for its quality real ales, traditional pub atmosphere and industrial setting in the heart of Kelham Island.

Dave was known for being a man of high standards, and incorporating those standards into everything he did. Now, Ed Wickett, current Pub Manager and Dave's son, is making sure to carry on his legacy. One of the biggest values Dave instilled in the business was to make it as inclusive as possible - open to all. Stepping inside on a Friday night, you'd probably see a group of 18 year olds in one corner and pensioners in the other. "It's fantastic that we get such a wide, varied customer base," Ed says. The pub prides itself on its recognisable and unchanged aesthetic. Customers will walk in and exclaim at the sense of nostalgia that hits them - "People tell you these stories about how they used to drink in here 15 years ago and it's not changed a bit, and they love that," Ed says. "And we love to hear that."

That being said, the team makes sure to keep up with modern trends and have recently added 50 gins behind the bar, after having none, to keep their customers satisfied - both new and existing. It's easy to see how the pub is still thriving after 40 years!

SHEFFIELD FLOOD 11th March 1864
WATER HEIGHT

SHEFFIELD FLOOD 25th June 2007
WATER HEIGHT

# INDUSTRY TAP

85 Sidney St, Sheffield City Centre, Sheffield S1 4RG

@Industrytapsheffield

*"Whether you're a matchday reveller or a beer ticking connoisseur, there's a beer for everyone at this truly independent Sidney Street boozer..."*

It's all about choice at the Industry Tap. Whether you're a matchday reveller or a beer ticking connoisseur, there's a beer for everyone at this truly independent Sidney Street boozer, and maybe even the odd surprise along the way too.

And when we say a beer for everyone, we mean there's a whopping 21 lines of choice! This staggering number of lines, plus fridges stacked full of bottles and cans, means you'd be hard pushed to find a better stocked bar anywhere in the city.

Showcasing brews from some of the world's finest craft beer brands, as well as local and UK-wide gems, the dog-friendly bar has you well-covered whether you're looking for a heady hit of hops, something a little lighter on the palate, or even an alcohol-free offering.

They also boast a wide selection of gin if that's more your thing, and if that wasn't enough, just to make sure they have all the bases covered, they even make sure there's always a top-quality, premium lager on draught.

"We'll always have a lager on," explains Industry Tap owner Darren Filsell. "There will always be someone who comes in not having tried craft beer before, so we always have one on because it's important to us that we cater for everyone."

Their veritable smorgasbord of choice on draught means they easily achieve this. A glance up at the two screens, which hang above the bar, can on any given day have details of stouts or imperial stouts, IPAs or double IPAs, sours and even premium ciders, on occasion.

**Speciality:**
**Dog-friendly**
**Try: the range of sours**

Within their broad range of styles, local breweries are well represented with Sheffield favourites like Abbeydale, Triple Point, Little Mesters and SMOD all getting a look in alongside industry darlings like DEYA, and even more unusual fare from further afield.

"We try to keep things a little bit different to everyone else," says Darren, "There's only so many beer suppliers and there's a few places all vying for similar sorts of beers, but I'm very big on working with breweries direct and trying to get stuff that's not been in Sheffield before.

"For example, I recently brought Campervan down from Leith, Scotland, which had never been seen south of Edinburgh before. That's what craft beer is about, for me. You have a passion for it, so when I want to try something new, I'll get it into the bar.

Darren and his knowledgeable team's passion make for a welcoming experience in the bar on the corner of Sidney Street, where Niche nightclub once enjoyed its heyday, and they've learned a lot in the short time since opening their doors in 2019.

Originally set up as a partnership between Darren and Mick and Lesley of Lost Industry, they parted ways in June 2020, but the bar continues to have a good relationship with the brewery and plenty of their excellent North Sheffield beers can still be found behind the bar, as well as pretty much anything else you might want to get your hands on.

We all have plenty of choices to make in life but visiting the Industry Tap bar is definitely one that you won't regret!

# THE ITCHY PIG

495 Glossop Rd, Sheffield S10 2QE
@Theitchypig

*Behind the bar you'll find a rotating cast of five hand pull cask lines and one cider, as well as four guest keg lines, which have all helped it be crowned West Sheffield's CAMRA Pub of the Year two years on the trot.*

**Speciality: Traditional real ales**

**Sheffield has undergone what you could call a micro-revolution when it comes to pubs, with several pint-sized venues springing up across the city, proving that good things do come in small packages, at least when it comes to top notch beer establishments.**

With the arrival of The Beer House, Walkley Beer Co. and Portland House in quick succession the city was awash with cosy drinking spots serving up quality beers from independent breweries, and chief among those trailblazers was The Itchy Pig, in Broomhill, which opened its doors in 2016.

The idea for the Glossop Road pub was conceived by owner Ted Finley while having a pint with his dad in his hometown of Faversham.

Ted explains: "The Itchy Pig was the dream. I'd recently moved to Sheffield with my girlfriend but struggled for work as a joiner. One day I was sat in this micropub with my dad when I thought, 'I could do this', and my dad went, 'go on then', and so the dream became reality."

In that period of early development, Ted thought the pub, which takes its name from his love of pork scratchings, would operate as a student hangout, given its location, but from very early on it was apparent that this wasn't going to be the case. Ted's love of real ales has meant that the venue has cornered the market for quality cask and keg beers in the area, with people travelling from miles around just to sample the different beers on offer.

While the pub may be small, measuring a cosy 8m by 4m, the beer selection is big, with a strong focus on real ales. Behind the bar you'll find a rotating cast of five hand pull cask lines and one cider, as well as four guest keg lines, which have all helped it be crowned West Sheffield's CAMRA Pub of the Year two years on the trot.

"Traditional real ales are our calling card," says Ted. "We also offer the friendliest service we possibly can and I think that goes a long way with a lot of people."

We've got a really loyal group of regulars who come in week in, week out, and I think that's because we cater for everyone. If you're looking for a good pint we tend to have something on that will tickle everyone's taste buds.

"We love what we do. That's the key thing, we all absolutely love our job and the city."

Ted loves the city so much in fact, that he even has plans to open a second venue, but for now he and his team are focused on delivering great beers and great service in their little corner of the Steel City.

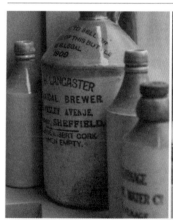

> **"**
> **ALL
> BARTENDERS ARE
> REALLY IS GLORIFIED
> CLEANERS WHO PUT
> STUFF IN CUPS, BUT
> I'D LIKE TO THINK I'VE
> PUT ENOUGH EFFORT
> INTO GOING ABOVE
> AND BEYOND AND
> REALLY LEARNING
> THE CRAFT.**
> **"**

# JOHN WICKHAM

# MIXIN' IT UP

*Over the last few years, Sheffield has become home to even more of the finest cocktail bars in the country, with the likes of Public, Pina and Bamboo Door popping up with menus full of cracking cocktails in cutting edge venues. With these new venues added to some old favourites, there's plenty of choice when it comes to quaffing the finest margaritas, martinis and mojitos but, as wonderful as the surroundings and drinks menus may be, venues still owe a huge debt of gratitude to the elite tier of cocktail slingers and mixologists we proudly boast in this city. So we had a chat with one of the best in the biz...*

They say good cocktail making is an art form and that's probably why The Parrot Club's John Wickham has made the transition from jazz pianist to cocktail maker so expertly. The seeds for this change in career were sewn while John was working part time at The Head of Steam in Huddersfield Train Station, his first bartending gig, while studying music at the University of Huddersfield.

The job hit all the right notes for John but he admits it was initially just a way to leave university without loads of debt (like everyone else, he did anyway). Explaining how he became hooked, John said: "I started doing the Belgian beer buying at The Head of Steam and got really into the geeky side of brewing. From there, I ended up in a couple of cocktail bars and just fell in love with it. I mean, all bartenders are really is glorified cleaners who put stuff in cups, but I'd like to think I've put enough effort into going above and beyond and really learning the craft."

John has been learning his craft for around a decade now, moving to Sheffield while his wife was completing a teaching degree in that time. Once in Sheff, he began working at former Ecclesall Road private members club,

The Pointing Dog, before moving on to become a manager at Cubanas, which is where he really honed his cocktail making skills, helping the party bar win best rum menu in the UK at the Golden Rum Barrel awards.

Nowadays, John can be found running the bar at the 'epic' and extremely popular Kelham Island cocktail venue, The Parrot Club. If you're into beautifully made cocktails, hip-hop and palm trees (and why wouldn't you be?) this is definitely the place for you.

The Parrot Club is also the home of another Sheffield fave, O'Hara's Spiced Rum and its premium sister brand, Sairen, and in recent times John has moved away from bartending full time, concentrating on his role developing rums for the in-house brands, but he is still known to pop on the apron from time to time and rustle up the odd mai tai, which he tells us is favourite drink to make.

With a packed out bar every weekend and new rums and spirits in development, the future looks rosy for John and The Parrot Club, and who knows, maybe one day he'll realise his ultimate dream of opening a jazz bar, where he can tinkle the ivories while serving the drinks.

# PARROT CLUB

Wincle Beer Company, Toll Barn, Wincle, SK11 0QE

**@parrotclubbar**

*Kelham Island has more than its fair share of amazing pubs and bars; whether it be real ale stalwarts harking back to the area's industrial heritage or trailblazers of its recent reinvigoration as one of the coolest spots in the city, there's a bit of something for everyone in the ever-expanding boundaries of Kelham, but there's really nothing else quite like the Parrot Club.*

Situated at 92 Burton Road, just next door to the warehouse which houses popular street food market Peddler, The Parrot Club is a late-night cocktail bar specialising in beautifully made cocktails, hip hop and erm... palm trees!

I mean, what's not to like, eh? Despite a rocky start to life, opening just months before venues were forced to close due to the pandemic, they've built quite the following in their relatively short life and are regularly fully booked for the entire weekend, as word spreads about the amazing cocktails and sumptuous surroundings.

The secret to Parrot Club's success is quite simply superb ingredients and an incredible team headed up by managers Tim Harrison and Katie Cooper, who both boast many years in the industry and the passion to boot. Tim said: 'I just love the idea of getting an incredible drink made with top tier ingredients but not having to be in a pretentious speak-easy to do it. Our laid back attitude and welcoming customer service is what sets us apart. Our drinks are simple, yet delicious and we highlight the point of each spirit before going overboard. Finally, our music! Smashing a Gibson Martini while west coast hip-hop is shouting all around me is my idea of heaven."

The bar is also the home of another Sheffield fave, O'Hara's Spiced Rum, and its new sister premium rum brand, Sairen. O'Hara's has been a Sheffield favourite for the best part of a decade, tantalising taste buds in Sheffield and beyond with classic rum flavours of vanilla, lime, cinnamon, cloves and a secret blend of spices. Sairen, however, is a different proposition altogether. A premium clear spiced rum that comes in three different varieties, Sairen is ideal for mixing top notch cocktails and is a bit more grown up; a perfect partner for Parrot Club cocktails.

Bar Owner and Head of Product Innovation John Wickham explains: "I'm

very proud of our Sairen rums. They're a natural, fresh and interesting addition to the spirit world bridging a gap of quality, elegance and accessibility from the rum and the gin market alike. We use them behind our bar and they are a pleasure to play with. Our bartenders love using them as they're super versatile, super mixable and just new and exciting."

The gorgeous drinks and attentive table service from knowledgeable staff complement the bar's luscious environment, making it the perfect place to enjoy anything from a special night out to a couple of cheeky after work piña coladas under the palm trees. Just make sure you book early.

# O'HARA'S SPICED RUM (37.5%)

**This Sheffield-based rum brand and its easily recognisable 'parrot bottles' have even been found on shores as far flung as Thailand and Vietnam.**

The story of O'Hara's Spiced Rum starts in 2009, when founder and namesake Andy O'Hara noticed a gap in the market for a vanilla-heavy spiced rum, after the market leader changed their recipe and moved away from using vanilla extract, as it became increasingly expensive.

Having spotted his opening, Andy worked with a flavour consultant to perfect the taste and balance of his own rum recipe, settling on a heady mix of Madagascan vanilla extract, cinnamon, a small amount of cloves, demerara sugar, which gives a toffee element to the rum, and finally, lime, which offers a bit of sharpness on the back of the palate.

Once they'd settled on this winning formula, the next challenge became sourcing the ingredients and working with a rum supply company along with an agent to undertake the laborious task of jumping through the required hoops to get the rum over to Blighty.

Once it had finally arrived, Sheffield went mad for it. Andy tells us that the demand was so high in those early days that it almost became impossible to keep up! Once they'd navigated that early period, selling the rum out of Andy's London Road pub The Cremorne, Andy took the brand to London and any Sheffield bar worth its salt (or sugar) began stocking the bottles.

Andy said: "It's a lovely drink and the number of people who say to me, the top comes off the bottle and it never goes back on, is just unreal, but then I get blamed for the hangover! People love it and the response has always been fantastic. It's just a flavour profile that people want to get on."

The rum remains as popular as ever, its successful rise uninterrupted since its launch, save for a short period in 2014 when the price of Madagascan vanilla extract skyrocketed to six times its usual value. Even the recent lockdowns didn't slow them down; instead it enabled them to explore even more of the rum sector, making a move into the premium rum market with new product Sairen, which uses high quality ingredients and beautiful packaging for an extra special tipple.

The branding is something that Andy knows is hugely important to the success of O'Hara's. People love the rum's taste, but they also love the iconic parrot on the side of the bottle, which was created by Sheffield artist Nick Deakin, whose enviable client list includes everything from local bars like Picture House Social, to global megabrand, Nike. His parrot design adorns t-shirts that, much like the rum itself, can now be found all over the world.

**oharasspiced.com**

# PIÑA

3 Harvest Ln, Neepsend, Sheffield S3 8EF

@pina.sheffield

**If you're looking for South Yorkshire's finest selection of quality mezcal, look no further than vibrant Mexican bar and restaurant piña.**

It all started with a journey that took Joe, the owner and founder, from Jalisco and Michoacán to Oaxaca and Mexico City, where he soon fell in love with the people, the culture and above all the cuisine.

The trip was financed by a tequila company so although it was drinks-led initially, Joe stayed on for another week to learn about not only the country's distilleries but its food, returning to bring a real taste of Mexico to Kelham Island.

The small but carefully curated cocktail list accompanies a much-loved taco menu, designed to introduce tequila and mezcal to the people of Sheffield. Joe hopes to enlighten people who think they hate the former spirit, having only drunk poor quality versions: unlike most varieties sold in the UK, at piña it's all 100% agave-based and of the highest quality.

"It's nice to know that we've become the place to get good tequila and mezcal in Sheffield, and people know what a good margarita tastes like now," says Joe.

The freshly made food and drinks, warm colours against exposed brickwork and relaxed ambience welcome everyone in at piña. Fusing the charm of their setting, an old warehouse in Sheffield's former industrial quarter, with the brightness of Mexican culture, spirits and cuisine has created a beautifully unique haven in the heart of the city.

# THE RUTLAND ARMS

86 Brown St, Sheffield City Centre, Sheffield S1 2BS

@rutlandarms

**In the centre of the city, a stone's throw from the station, The Rutland Arms is a proper pub. It takes that identity seriously indeed, from its classic jukebox (though there a few tongue-in-cheek house rules on what musn't be played) to its tempting selection of hand-pumps and fridges full of intriguing craft beers.**

It does everything a traditional pub should do, welcoming people of all generations (and their dogs, too) with friendly staff and a great pint.

The staff are self-professed beer lovers, and it's clear to see from the interesting selection on offer that they put an enormous amount of effort into choosing an array of drinks that is a little different to most other pubs. Local breweries are always well-represented on the bar, too, adding to a wonderful choice for punters who either get snug inside the cosy main room or take drinks to the suntrap beer garden out back.

If the 20 cask and keg taps and specialist bottled/canned offerings don't take your fancy, there's a well-stocked back bar offering pretty much everything else: wines, spirits, whisky, gin, rum, real ciders, and plenty of soft drinks. Expect to be watered and fed in style with an innovative pub grub menu that's revered throughout the city. An absolute all-rounder of a pub and a gem in the city's beery crown.

# SHAKESPEARES

146-148 Gibraltar St, Sheffield S3 8UB

@shakespearesshf

*...the pub was featured twice in The Guardian and once in The Times back in 2018, including being featured in The Guardian's round up of 'The 50 Best UK Pubs' for which Shakespeares came in the top 10 for best craft beers!*

**Speciality: Welcoming atmosphere**

Situated on the famous Don Valley real ale trail between Kelham Island and the city centre is Shakespeares – one of Sheffield's longest standing establishments. The pub itself has been around for 200 years, give or take a decade and has always been some form of inn or a resting stop for people to stay when they were travelling through. One of the rooms even used to be an alleyway into the beer garden where horses would be kept. Imagine drinking somewhere with all that rich history.

But enough about the then, let's talk about the now. Current owner, William Wagstaff, bought the pub in 2010 and after 18 months of closure for renovations, opened it again on the 21st of July, 2011 to be the Shakespeares people know and love today.

In that decade they've achieved plenty. As pub manager, one of the proudest moments for Chris Wadsworth was when the pub was featured twice in The Guardian and once in The Times back in 2018, including being featured in The Guardian's round up of 'The 50 Best UK Pubs' for which Shakespeares came in the top 10 for best craft beers! Another big achievement for the pub was being named by CAMRA as one of the best pubs in the country for four consecutive years from 2016 to 2019. Getting this recognition just proves to Chris and the team that they're doing something right for their customers.

You could say that the key to Shakespeares' success has been their approach to service. When you step inside you're instantly hit with the old worldly setting of the place, giving it a traditional feel that they've worked hard to keep. But then when it comes to ordering, they keep the bar up to date by stocking it with beverages that are bang on trend. Their main focus is their craft beer range, but they also offer plenty of other thirst-quenchers, including over one hundred whiskies.

If you're still in doubt as to why Shakespeares is the place to go, then be reassured by what Chris has to say:

"It may sound cheesy but we have worked hard to have an open and welcoming nature, provided by our great team of staff who get on with everyone, do the job, and create the atmosphere." But don't just take his word for it, several social media groups – including the Sheffield LGBTQIA+ group, have named Shakespeares as a welcoming and safe space, proving that the pub isn't just for 'mainstream drinkers' but for everyone!

Good beer at a good price, with good company – what more do you need?

# THE SHEAF VIEW

25 Gleadless Rd, Lowfield, Sheffield S2 3AA

@thesheafview

Part of the famed 'Heeley Triangle' – an enviable run of traditional boozers featuring The White Lion, The Brothers Arms and this renowned watering hole – The Sheaf View is a popular alehouse known for its generous real ale selection, showcasing an ever-rotating range of 8 cask ales, 3 guest kegs, a vast array of whiskies and spirits, alongside quality lagers, ciders and wheat beers.

Currently under the stewardship of the much-loved Neepsend Brew Co, you'll always be able to enjoy a fresh sup from their core range offering on the bar, or even take the opportunity to grab a 5L mini-keg for takeout. Homely and cosy on the inside with a surprisingly large beer garden out back serving as a perfect suntrap during the warmer months. The dogs of Sheffield love it here as well, always on-hand to sniff out a decent ale or two for the punters.

Sadly, the pub faced an arson attack in 2021, leaving it with no option to close due to extensive damage received to the historic building. Thankfully, fans of the pub rallied and donated almost £2,000 (at time of print) to help the venue get back on its feet – a testament of its value to the Sheffield community.

# TWO THIRDS BEER CO.

434-436 Abbeydale Road, Sheffield S7 1FQ

@twothirdsbeerco

In late 2018, over a round of cañas on one of Seville's rooftop bars, three mates from Sheffield set out to create a neighbourhood craft beer bar that was friendly, relaxed and served only the finest craft beers you could find.

Fast forward to November 2019 and the doors were open at Two Thirds Beer Co., boasting 16 rotating draught beer lines, a giant craft beer fridge showcasing over 100 different bottles and cans from around the world, as well as an eclectic line-up of spirits, wines, soft drinks and snacks to enjoy in a laidback and unpretentious environment.

They have transformed the former home of a vegan dessert shop into the ultimate modern but cosy hops paradise – with a warm, softly-lit interior, comfy snug booths and a giant glass frontage overlooking the bustling, bohemian stretch of Abbeydale Road. It's the perfect place to grab an interesting sup and watch the Steel City go by.

The bar proudly embraces the smaller than usual two thirds pint measure, encouraging visitors to sample a wider range of ever-changing craft beers and ciders. The concept emerged during the aforementioned trip owners Ben, Danny and Adam took to Seville, where the caña (a small glass of beer) is the standard serve for drinks. Naturally, good beer is of the highest importance, but the bar has a cracking line-up of gins which are served in their oft-admired retro gin balloons.

Situated right at the centre of Abbeydale Road's popular and vibrant independent quarter, the bar has fast become a favourite of both locals and beer enthusiasts alike. The indoor tables and popular European-style outdoor terrace are regularly packed on weekends and for post-work drinks, so heading down early is a must. If you're feeling peckish, street food specialists Get Wurst knock out banging bratwurst, currywurst and vegan wurst offerings all week from their kitchen. We'll raise a glass to that!

# SHEFFIELD TAP

1b Sheaf St, Sheffield City Centre, Sheffield S1 2BP
@thesheffieldtap

*The Tap has become one of the most popular pubs in the city since it opened 11 years ago. Stop in after work with colleagues, for a pre-match pint on a Saturday or simply to enjoy drinks with friends amidst Edwardian splendour.*

**Speciality: Mojo - A light-bodied session pale ale.**

As the first and final impression for many commuters in the Steel City, high standards at the Sheffield Tap have always been a top priority. Situated between Sheaf Street and Platform 1b at the train station, housed within the former Edwardian refreshment room and dining rooms, it's a uniquely quaint environment for a venue placed right in the middle of a lot of people's commutes.

The Tap opened in 2009 inside a restored Grade-II listed railway building. The interior is divided into two areas: the main bar, which was originally a drinking space for 'commoners', and a grand dining room for first class passengers. They're divided by a broad hallway that was originally open to the outside platform, but now form smaller, more intimate spaces.

The interior of the whole bar creates an atmosphere where everyone feels welcome and comfortable, whether you are with a group of friends out for a big night or simply enjoying a coffee while waiting for a train. The restored former first class dining room features a working micro-brewery, The Tapped Brew Co. It usually brews between two and three times a week, and if you like beer then you'll love the aroma of malt and hops wafting through the bar!

According to general manager Craig Chaplin, it's that proud commitment to providing a benchmark pubbing experience which has allowed the popular beer sanctuary to bounce back strongly following a difficult 2020 – with a snazzy new-look outdoor space to go with it.

"I think many places across the bar and pub community here in Sheffield are used to being dynamic.

"We have two universities with different freshers weeks, various big events running throughout the year, Tramlines, derby matches, varsity games, etc – so basically we're used to and are pretty good at changing things up. We're Yorkshire folk and we crack on and make do."

Feeding into the newly relaxed, continental feel is the addition of new seating and large biergarten-style brollies to provide some shade during sunny drinking sessions. Everything is spaced out according to government guidelines, and there's no need to leave your seat if you don't feel comfortable doing so.

If that's not enough to tempt you in, the Sheffield Tap was recently crowned the city centre's CAMRA Pub of the Year for its hard work pre-lockdown. Equipped as per usual with its wide range of world beers, craft offerings, on-site microbrewery and premium wine and spirit selection, it's the perfect spot for some social and secure summer fun.

The Tap (as it is affectionately referred to) was one of the first bars in Sheffield to showcase beers from around the world and the UK. Thornbridge Brewery has supported the venture from the start, so their locomotive nameplate is mounted in the entrance and you'll always find Jaipur on cask and extremely fresh!

The bar itself is so popular that a complaint often heard there is that when people come to Sheffield, they don't go any further than the Sheffield Tap: they plan to go out and visit lots of bars in town, but then they get here and don't leave! As a result, the pub has picked up the nickname the Sheffield Trap.

# RETAILERS

# THE BEAR

**A new addition to Sheffield's beer scene, The Bear opened its doors in June 2021, in the former home of the Rude Shipyard, on Abbeydale Road.**

Featuring six keg lines and a range of lagers, pale ales, IPAs, stouts, sours and ciders from a variety of local and national breweries, The Bear gives people plenty of choice to try in store, helping them make the right choice for the perfect set of cans and bottles to take away and enjoy at home.

"This is the key for me and what I envisioned when I was planning The Bear," says owner Matt Beety, "a place where people come in and sit and chat about the beers they've been drinking lately, and this helps me to guide them toward something suitable if they don't know what they want when they come in.

"Some days people come in alone for a drink or to choose some takeaway cans and will end up chatting to people on another table about their beer experiences, recommending something they have tried, or give me ideas of what they would like to see come in.

"Others like to just sit at the window shelves and watch the world go by on Abbeydale Road or sit out the front of the shop with something refreshing.

The layout and size of the room means that people often strike up conversations with Matt, or each other, and there has been a collective community feel to the space since it opened While Matt is really pleased to already be welcoming regular customers through the doors, people are still only just discovering the wonders inside and popping in to check it out.

One prominent Sheffield brewer who visited shortly after opening told Matt there were things they had never seen before in the city. "I try to stock some surprises, as well as local and national favourites," explains Matt, "so this was good to hear.

"We are very lucky in Sheffield to have four of our best breweries dedicated to making top class gluten-free beer. Abbeydale, Triple Point, Crosspool Ale Makers and Little Mesters all feature in the kegs and fridges and help provide a really accessible offer, with the Little Mesters lager and Triple Point NEIPA and IPA being some of the most popular."

As well as a focus on gluten-free beer, many of the products are also vegan, and Matt even stocks a brewery who bore their own water and produce

their own electricity to power their brewing processes.

Matt is trying to stock as diverse a range of beers as possible. He said: "There are black-owned and African inspired breweries, and a brewery who support LGBTQ+ charities from their sales on the shelves, and they are all producing fantastic beer at the same time.

"I also support a few very small breweries, locally and nationally, including some who have never sent beer to Sheffield before."

The shop stocks over 150 individual beers now, and regulars have commented on how varied the selection is, with a large range of pales and IPAs taking up most of the fridge space, local and European lagers, a growing, fruity selection of sours and ciders, and no and low alcohol beers.

A large range of stouts and porters fill the shelves on the opposite side of the shop, and beers range from just £2 up to £9, with just about every kind of flavour and style within the beer spectrum on offer.

So, if you go down to The Bear today, you may be in for a big surprise!

# BEER CENTRAL

Outlet MS3, The Moor Market, Sheffield S1 4PF
@beercentralsheff

**Set within the Moor Market, Beer Central is Sheffield's busiest city-centre beer shop, where a friendly approach to customer service is the order of the day.**

Sean Clarke first had the idea to open his own shop while in the place where most good ideas are formed... the pub. One evening back in 2012, while sitting in The Sheffield Tap, Sean was bemoaning the city centre's lack of places to buy smart beers to take home. This was at the same time as the new Moor Market was due to open, so he said goodbye to his job as a teacher and decided to give it a go himself. Despite the whirlwind effort of getting everything ready, Sean and co-owner Deborah Jackson opened Beer Central on the same day the market opened its doors in November 2013. The subsequent years have brought great success, a string of awards and a band of loyal customers who really do make it all worthwhile. "Selling beer and chatting to amazing people really is a dream job and we love every minute of every day, always feeling lucky to do what we do," says Sean.

Today Beer Central stocks 350+ beers that range from traditional classics to new and unusual rare offerings. "We don't play it safe when choosing stock, so we tend to have things that other outlets might not consider," he explains. "We like to have the right drink for whoever walks through our doors, whether it's someone looking for a local Best Bitter or a craft beer enthusiast wanting to try the latest IPA or Imperial Stout." The business uses social media extensively to keep in touch with its customers. People keep an eye on what comes in and then they request a beer or two to be added to their order box. The box can then remain at the shop as they keep adding to it whenever new things arrive, so they end up with a totally personalised box of beer that is ready when they are. The ultimate in simplicity, convenience and choice, this system has won over hundreds of beer-lovers across the city and beyond.

With a city-centre location that is hard to beat, customer-focused flexibility and the very best tipples you can get, Beer Central is playing a strong role in keeping Sheffield firmly on the British beer map.

PRICED ON TOP

£3·50

TOP

PRICED ON TOP

# DRAM SHOP

21 Commonside, Sheffield S10 1GA
@thedramshopuk

Located in leafy Walkley, The Dram Shop is one of the area's most trusted alcohol sellers. They have a loyal customer base, having been around since 1982, and specialise in innovative Yorkshire brewed beers. Dram Shop has been run by Tony, his wife and their two children since 2005 when the previous owner retired. Tony's wife had already worked in the shop for over 15 years, and said it seemed a shame to let such a community-loved business die, so they took over!

Tony says he's always working – whether that be when he's out for a meal and spots a new beer for the shop or when he's thinking of ways to reach more people and give them a divine drinking experience. He's seen the alcohol industry change so much since he entered the profession and says how he likes to think that they're selling "not beers, but experiences", just for the sheer amount of variety that is now available. More homegrown goodness means supporting the local economy and community,

two things which Dram Shop keep at its core.

The shop specialises in Sheffield-based beer, with close links to breweries such as Abbeydale, Bradfield and Little Critters, but also has a wide range of Yorkshire, European and American beers. A particular favourite is Sam Smiths, brewed in the county and a sure-fire seller. The range of craft IPAs is immense – from Wilde Child's 'Brownie Huntress' and 'Chasing Epiphany' to Black Iris' 'Endless Summer' and 'Divine Element', the shop has over 150 cans in store ready for you to sample.

The shop also sells wine and spirits, with one of their most popular products being whisky. You can find aged whiskies such as the 18 year old sherry cask aged Arran Single Malt Scotch Whisky and gins such as Two Birds Watermelon Gin in store.

Welcoming to students and the wider community alike, Dram Shop has been a staple in Walkley for 40 years, and with Tony and his family's passion for good drink experiences, it seems set to stay.

# HOP HIDEOUT

Unit 11, Kommune, 1-13 Angel St, Sheffield S3 8LN

@hophideout

pic: Mark Newton

Founded by Jules Gray in 2013 as a 'labour of beery love', Hop Hideout is an award-winning speciality beer shop and tasting room that's home to an increasingly eclectic selection of craft beers, ciders and wines. Jules has always been passionate about beer; after working at a brewery and later becoming a regular blogger about the subject for Exposed Magazine, it seemed the natural next step to launch her own independent beery business.

Originally starting in the back of an antiques centre on Abbeydale Road in Sheffield's Antiques Quarter before moving into a nearby café space, since 2019 Hop Hideout can be found within the wonderful walls of Kommune food hall. Situated in the city centre on the site of the Grade II listed former Co-Op building, it's in prime position for people to come and browse the 200+ chilled beers on display.

One of the first 'drink in' beer shops in the UK, the wide selection of beers are available to enjoy there and then or takeaway – including four fresh rotating draught taps. Such is the variety on offer,

it's guaranteed you'll find something right up your street. Jules herself has a particular penchant for wild ales, funky beers, natural wines and farmhouse ciders.

There's a genuine sense of community around the shop, which holds regular events such as Meet the Brewers as well as beer and food matching tasting sessions, while on a slightly more active note Hop Hideout hosts the monthly Sheffield chapter of the global Mikkeller Running Club. Jules is passionate about Sheffield, good causes, and making beer a welcoming space for everyone. She is also the founder of annual city-wide beer event Sheffield Beer Week and independent craft beer festival Indie Beer Feast.

With a curated range of quality ciders nestled in alongside natural wines and a craft beer offering from around the world, Jules has built a reputation as a national beer expert and hosted beer tastings on commercial TV and radio as well as featuring on podcasts such as Beer With Nat and Good Beer Hunting. Hop Hideout has also picked up accolades such as Independent Beer Retailer of the Year (2018) and Ratebeer.com Best Bottleshop in South Yorkshire (2019).

pic: Mark Newton

# BEER REVERE

*Jules Gray went from blogging about the local beer scene to becoming a driving force in its development. In 2013, she opened specialist beer and cider shop Hop Hideout before going on to found Sheffield Beer Week in 2015 and its sister event Indie Beer Feast in 2019. Today Jules continues to work hard promoting independent businesses in the beer industry, which led to the co-ordination of Indie Beer Shop Day in 2021, a nationwide event which saw over 100 independent shops uniting to celebrate the sector through a range of activities and collaborations. We spoke to Jules about her journey from beer blogger to business owner and how she sees the future panning out for the beer industry in the Steel City.*

**Tell us a bit about yourself and how you first became involved in the local beer industry?**

I came to study in Sheffield in the late 1990s and always enjoyed the city's friendly, welcoming vibe. Unfortunately due to work opportunities outside of the city I ended up moving away. After working in the beer trade at various pubs, clubs and then a brewery, I returned to live in Sheffield around 2011, deciding to commute out for work.

At the time I was blogging as a hobby about beer, beer and food pairing, pubs, breweries and homebrewing. I came across Sheffield's Exposed Magazine and wondered whether there'd be room for a beer column to expand on my passion for writing and beer, which they kindly told me there was! So visiting Sheffield's beer hotspots became frequent and I found myself more deeply involved in the scene.

**Where did the inspiration for Hop Hideout first come from?**

Around 2012 I was becoming tired from commuting, stressed from working on a big systems implementation project at the brewery I was at and generally a little unhappy. Then, in 2013, I attended a European Beer Bloggers Conference in Edinburgh and met a few folks working in the independent and newly forming craft beer sector. I guess it was

at that point I started to research and think of ways I could transition from the macro brewing world to the independent beer sector. Back then there wasn't a huge selection of jobs available in the sector, especially on the doorstep. So it was sort of inevitable I had to start my own business. I'd thought about opening a micropub and had spoken to Martyn Hillier (now Chair of Micropub Association). Though I loved cask ale, I was always passionate about Belgian, US and world beer, plus the growing new UK breweries like The Kernel Brewery. So a beer shop with a drink-in tasting room element, like many places in Belgium, became my focus.

**What are the main challenges facing local breweries and specialist beer shops today?**

Rising costs of rent, services, cost of goods and beer; having to diversify revenue streams, which impacts the workload of an already generally small and stretched team; macro breweries buying 'craft' beer brands and using their marketing budgets and influence to gain space in the market over the original craft breweries that created the beers and the space; the driving down of pricing in the sector by supermarkets, often funded by huge marketing deals from big brands; the control of the vast majority of the beer market by a

# JULES GRAY

handful of huge brewing and pub companies. All these elements make it a challenging trade to be involved with, but often these are mirrored in many other sectors too!

**Just how important are indie beer shops to local communities and supplementing a city's wider beer scene in general?**

Huge, I believe, as they're places of discovery and gateways for people to learn about and enjoy beer. They're community hubs to meet other passionate enthusiasts. They certainly keep many local high streets vibrant and busy with footfall, as other retail units around them fold and close, in addition to boosting local breweries' profiles and revenue by buying and promoting their beers. It's a very closely intertwined symbiotic relationship.

**What are the biggest changes you've seen since you first began blogging on the Sheffield beer scene?**

Sheffield, to me, has seemed fairly slow and organic in growth and change. I think there's certainly more variety on offer in terms of good beer places to drink in, which is great, and that includes traditional pubs and bars, drink-in beer shops, micropubs and brewery taprooms. It's also brilliant to see the diversity of beer styles available, from beautiful cask pale ales to tasty keg-dispensed IPAs, sour beers and more.

**Sheffield Beer Week has become one of, if not the, most important dates on the city's beery calendar. Can you talk us through your journey with the event and some of your proudest moments so far?**

That's such a difficult one to choose as there have been so many superb memories over the six years. Though year six, in 2021, was a virtual celebration due to the coronavirus pandemic – so we'll brush past that one! After being inspired by many beer weeks in the US and Norwich City of Ale, I thought: why hasn't such a great beer city as Sheffield got something similar, to positively

shout about its scene and connect with the wider global beer landscape?

The first Sheffield Beer Week launched in 2015 just a couple of months before the March event date – still very much an idea and social media campaign. Initially, venues and breweries were a little apprehensive, but we had a good response from a handful. This enabled us to go ahead and I think once others saw the positives and the good response from consumers it blossomed and grew. There are now roughly 40 venues and over 80 events on a typical year. Beer and food pairings events are some of my favourites: Wild Beer Co a The Stag, Boozy Brunch at The Rutland Arms and beer writer Mark Dredge's paired menu and talk at Triple Point have all been fantastic. We even had a group of 15 Scandinavian brewers visit one year, which was wonderful to see; they were really interested to discover how cask ale i brewed and packaged. I've also really enjoyed getting involved in a number of the key beer week organic strands, such as hosting women in bee and brewing celebrations and talks with folk like FemAle and Ladies That Beer. The Photography Trail we hosted across a number o venues (Hop Hideout, Sheffield Tap, Kelhan Island Brewery Bar, The Rutland, Shakespeares with Nicci Peet and Mark Newton was reall powerful to see exhibited in place – showcasin the people in the beer industry and drinkers. Oh also Steve Hindy, one of the founders of Brookly Brewery, hosting a fireside chat on his birthday a Thornbridge's Hallamshire House was a ver special beery moment in time.

**Why do you think Sheffield enjoys such a thriving beer community? How do yo see this developing in the future?**

Sheffield really supports independents acros most sectors, particularly food, drink, music an arts. I think that's a really positive starting poin I do think it's an affordable city to live in and tha does help to some degree with disposable incom

and folks being able to shop and drink local. Generally, there's a friendly, competitive nature within the independent beer community so many people will help each other out and collaborate.

I'd like to see more diversification of people in the industry and drinkers; I think that could bring hugely exciting, thriving and interesting elements. I'd like to see more places champion campaigns like the Everyone Welcome Initiative and Know The Line Campaign. It'd be great to see more brewery cross-collabs outside of the sector – I'm really intrigued by cider/beer and wine/beer hybrids.

**Personally, what are your goals for Hop Hideout, Indie Beer Feast and Sheffield Beer Week in the coming years?**

Such a big question! I'm certainly interested in opening another neighbourhood branch of Hop Hideout alongside the foodhall location – maybe with some additional elements, but I can't share too much on that. Indie Beer Feast is organically growing along with the venue; it's an historic 1920s building undertaking lots of structural work, so the more they open or do it up, it allows more spaces for us to utilise for things like pop-up tastings and content for the event. Sheffield Beer Week wouldn't be what it is without the venues and folks involved really, so a big thanks to everyone who gets inspired and involved each year. Because of this, to a degree, it can be very spontaneous in terms of what actually happens, but this is why it keeps such a good energy year in, year out. We've collaborated with other city's beer weeks – like our close Norwich links and I'd really like to do more of those, too. It all shows the wonderfully unifying nature of beer.

**@beer_revere**

# MITCHELLS WINE MERCHANTS

354 Meadowhead, Sheffield S8 7UJ
@mitchellswine

*Sheffield runs in Mitchell's blood, and the family really are built into the brickwork of the city. His great-grandfather, Henry Sampson, owned a pub back in the 1860s called Adelphi, which was where Sheffield Wednesday and Yorkshire Cricket were founded.*

**Mitchells Wine Merchants is an integral part of Sheffield's retail community, and their name has been known in Meadowhead for over 85 years.**

The departmental store is run by John Mitchell, his daughter Frankie – the third generation of the family to do so – and her husband James. Mitchell's grandfather was a publican at the George IV pub on Infirmary Road when he sent his son, Dennis, to Henry Fanshawe School in Dronfield. On Dennis' journey into school, a row of shops in Meadowhead would often catch his eye. He went on to be an apprentice butcher before eventually opening his own butchers there in 1935 on the very same row of shops. In 1961, the family moved out of the living quarters inside the shop and Mitchell's father refurbished it into a beer-off, later to become the wine merchants and Aladdin's cave of treats it is today, thereby opening a new chapter in the life of the family. The address they continue to operate out of today is 352 and 354 Meadowhead: 354 being the 3000 sq. ft departmental store, and 352 being Little Mesters Microbrewery & Mitchells Tasting Room.

Sheffield runs in Mitchell's blood, and the family really are built into the brickwork of the city. His great-grandfather, Henry Sampson, owned a pub back in the 1860s called Adelphi, which was where Sheffield Wednesday and Yorkshire Cricket were founded. The pub was pulled down in 1970 and replaced by the famous Crucible Theatre, and even further back down their line of Steel City ancestors is Thomas Boulsover, who invented the Sheffield plate.

The merchants are highly regarded throughout Yorkshire, winning a huge number of awards including Wine Merchant of the Year twice, and the same in the beer and spirit categories. The heavily stocked cabinets feature 800+ whiskies from around the world – from your everyday drinking bottle to the best of the best, limited editions, collectables and one-offs. The store includes fridges lined with 1000+ beers – 500 of which are craft brews, 300+ English bottled ales and 300+ ready chilled world beers with a special focus on those from Germany. Throw in 75+ vodkas, 100+ rums, 60+ Cognacs, Armagnacs and brandies, 200+ cocktails, liqueurs and aperitifs – plus an expanding tequila, agave and mezcal collection in the works.

Mitchells also holds an impressive selection of Havana cigars; spread over five fabulous humidors they stand as the second largest specialist retailer of Havanas in the north. But it's not just about the Havanas: their selection includes many from around the globe from the Dominican to Nicaragua, Holland to Honduras.

Wines and champagnes are very much at the forefront of the store, with over 1500 from all around the world and a key focus on diversity, whilst refreshing the selection all the time and keeping up with the trends. Non-alcoholic wines of quality have seen a rise for those following a healthier lifestyle, not to mention the popularity of natural unfiltered wines and orange wines, both of which have sporadic bottle fermentation and offer a different take

on a classic bottle of wine. If there is something new that you're looking for but not quite sure, their 16-bottle Enomatic wine machines facilitate the option to freely try before you buy, encouraging customers to step outside comfort zones and expand palates. Even considering the ever-changing world of wine, Mitchells will never neglect the best-sellers that have lined their shelves for over 40 years. A wine for every occasion is the ethos here.

All things tasting is the way to go these days, and above the brewery they have a specialised tasting room and museum holding memorabilia collected over the last 50 years. The tasting room itself holds 35 people, and Mitchells run 2-3 tasting events every month. With gin and whisky by far being the most popular, they bring in distillers, producers and ambassadors from all around the UK and across the globe. The intimate venue has hosted some fabulous evenings with the likes of Torres Wines from Spain, Babich Wines of New Zealand, John Cherry of Sir Robin of Locksley

Gin, Pol Roger Champagne, Hugel Wines of Alsace and Nikka Japanese Whisky, Paul John Whiskies of Goa and Mackmyra Whiskies of Sweden – just to mention a few!

From starting as a small family business to most recently delivering far and wide, Mitchell's continues to achieve. Sending out orders both locally and nationally, they have made it easier for everyone to try their wines, bringing the fun straight to your doorstep. With such an illustrious history and unique array of products, their place in Sheffield is firmly secured, and John hopes that the family will continue to bring some of life's biggest pleasures to the locals of the city for more generations to come.

Mitchells would like to thank you all for you continued loyalty, supporting local independents and keeping Sheffield's scene thriving.

# PANGOLIN CRAFT BEER SHOP

80 Middlewood Rd, Hillsborough, Sheffield S6 4HA

@pangolin_craft_beer

Heading up a revitalisation of the Hillsborough drinking scene, especially when it comes to craft beer, is The Pangolin – a bar and craft beer shop situated on Middlewood Road. Joining the bar along the same stretch in recent years are micropubs Northern Monkey and Brass Monkey, combining to make the area a newly attractive proposition for craft ale drinkers.

Pangolin – named after owner Nick Davy's favourite animal – offers three cask and five keg lines, as well as a carefully curated selection of beers, wines and premixed spirits that can be enjoyed inside the relaxed, cosy venue, or you can grab an interesting takeout or two from the large fridge and shelving to the side of the bar.

Nick, a long-term Hillsborough resident and former member of the popular Walkley Beer Co, opened the bar in 2020 and quickly turned it into a hoppy hub of delights specialising in modern UK craft beers sourced locally and nationally. Beyond that, there's a selection of international beers from America and Canada, the best of new European craft beers, along with more traditional European styles such as German and Czech pilsners, plus a fine mixture of Weiss beers and some high-quality Belgian ales.

# TURNER'S BOTTLE SHOP

298 Abbeydale Rd, Nether Edge, Sheffield S7 1FL
@turnersbottleshop

Turner's Bottle shop and Tap Room has been a part of the Sheffield craft beer community for the past six years, nestled amongst a vibrant mix of independent business, they form a part of the ever expanding, thriving food and drinks scene on Abbeydale Road.

Over the six years, owners Alison and Rob have seen the business grow organically from a craft beer-centered bottle shop to a drinks emporium and tap room bar with the ethos that craft and artisan drinks should be accessible to all. As such, they aim to create a welcoming environment for everyone, from the beer enthusiast searching out the latest releases, to those who want something a little different but are not quite sure where to look and need a friendly approachable guide.

Alison explains: "Specialist shops can feel a little intimidating and we want to break down those barriers, creating a place where people can come in and feel comfortable, with a wide range of products to suit all tastes and budgets."

The bottle shop is filled with over 400 different lines, featuring beers and cider from around the world, and guaranteeing you can find a new favourite beer each time you visit. As Sheffield is blessed to have a plethora of great breweries in the city they are proud to feature these local beers on their shelves.

If beer on tap is more your thing, then you've gone to the right place. They currently boast eight tap lines and offer beer to go in Growlers; these are one litre glass bottles using a counter-pressure filling system which makes sure the beer stays fresh for up to three weeks. This system uses the same technology as some microbreweries use to bottle their beer at the brewery. The filler floods the growler with carbon dioxide, creating a pressurised environment free of oxygen that prevents the beer from oxidising. If you like your beer sustainable then this is the perfect option, fill, drink, return, repeat!

It's not just beer either, there is natural and low intervention wine on offer, including wine from one of the most northerly vineyards in England. The collection of artisanal and small batch spirits is curated from local distillers, handpicked to ensure quality. Continuing the theme of inclusivity there is also a wide range of lo/no alcohol beers alongside a great selection of gluten-free and vegan options. Can't decide what to take away? Everything is also available to drink in, either in the cosy tap room bar or outside watching the world go by. What are you waiting for?

## DEAN HOLLINGWORTH

# THE RETURN OF STONES

**In 2020 True North Brew Co. officially announced their brewery team would be heading up the revival of Stones Bitter.**

This was much to the delight of beer drinkers up and down the country, but no more so than those native to Sheffield itself. Stones hadn't been brewed in Sheffield for 21 years after the original brewery closed in 1999, but as of April 2021 it's back, and just as good as people remember. When asked what prompted this resurrection Dean Hollingworth, head brewer at True North Brew Co. said: "We had always wanted to revive a lost Sheffield beer, and we were already working closely with Molson Coors who own the brand, so it was the perfect opportunity for us both to resurrect such an iconic Sheffield brand and return it to its birthplace."

From the start of the process, Dean had said that he wanted to bring the beer back up to its original cask strength of 4.1%. He also wanted to use the original yeast which gave it its unique flavour. "I was lucky enough to have access to the original brew sheets," Dean says. "And the famous Sheffield Cannon yeast was still being used in Tadcaster, so we were able to get it pretty much as it was brewed back in the day."

The return was a lot more than Dean initially expected. "I got really overwhelmed at how much nostalgia it evoked in people all over the country," he says. "We were bombarded with emails of people's memories of their first pints or how it reminded them of grandparents. Everyone seemed to have a story about Stones Bitter."

Being under the watchful eye of the brand owners (and what felt like the whole of Sheffield) the brewing team made sure they stuck to the original recipe word for word. Dean even managed to contact some of the old brewers and get the water profile exactly as it was down at the Neepsend Cannon Brewery. He described it as a nervewracking evening when the old brewers went to the brewery for a sample and to sign it off before the team could officially release it. Luckily they gave it the thumbs up! When it came time to begin building the anticipation in the beer community for the big return, True North Brew Co. didn't have to do much; there really are a lot of Stones fans out there! Everyone was more than ready. Although True North's marketing manager still did a great job generating a palatable sense of homecoming hype culminating in a launch party at the Riverside pub. And now the brewery, and Dean personally, consider bringing Stones back to Sheffield their biggest achievement – and what an achievement, eh?

# STONES (4.1%)

**The most famous beer ever made in Sheffield has its roots in the vast factories and mills that helped the city build a reputation as an industrial powerhouse.**

Stones Bitter was first brewed at the Cannon Brewery, Neepsend, in 1948 by William Stones Ltd, and was initially designed with the local steelworkers in mind. The beer's original recipe and its water content included extra minerals to replenish those the workers lost during long, arduous shifts in the factories.

The growing popularity of bitter in the 1940s and 50s made it an immediate huge success. By the 1960s the beverage had become known as 'more of a religion than a beer' across South Yorkshire, which led to Bass Brewery, one of the UK's largest national breweries at the time, buying William Stones in 1968 and opened the beer up to a nationwide audience. Its rise throughout the 1980s was meteoric and Stones became the UK's highest selling bitter in 1992; but its widened commercial appeal saw a number of significant changes made, which included changing the original recipe to achieve a lower percentage ABV (a cost-saving exercise) and production beginning to move away from the original Sheffield site. In 1999, due in part to the prioritisation of its Carling and Worthington's brands, Cannon Brewery was closed and Stones was never brewed in the city again.

That is until 2020, when Sheffield craft brewery True North Brew Co announced they would be re-brewing the iconic beverage in its original cask ale form, taking it back up to 4.1% ABV and sticking closely to the original recipe using original yeast strains and water recipes from the 1970s. The bitter made its return with a launch in April 2021 and continues to be brewed at True North's city centre brewery – an ode to the classic brand and its roots. It has a fragrant grapefruit-citrus hop aroma, which cuts through a characteristically sulphury background with a fruity edge. The unusual salt balance ensures that the bitterness isn't dry. Stones would go perfectly with a Ploughman's lunch – after all, bitters work wonderfully with cheese, meat pies and cooked meats... all the components of a local pub classic!

**truenorthbrewco.uk**

TRUE
NORTH
BREW CO

There's no plac
like Stones.

Established 1865
Returning April 2020

Iconic Brews

STONES

Stones

Stones
Best
Bitter

# BEER EVENTS

**With such a rich history of beer and brewing, it's no surprise there are some fantastic beer events in the city...**

## Sheffield Beer Week

Given Sheffield's long history of brewing, it's no surprise that Sheffield Beer Week is a cause for much collaboration across the city. Embracing the past and future of beer culture in the city, the week-long festival throws open the doors of breweries and bars alike, allowing visitors to get a look at the whole story; from grains to drained pints.

Since its inaugural event in 2015 the 'week' has grown rapidly in size, bringing together 40 venues and 60 events across 10 days in 2019. Whilst casting a loving eye over Sheffield's brewing pedigree through open days at local breweries, the festival also looks forward, pushing new tastes and bringing in fresh custom to the local industry.

In 2017, there were six special collaborations and 'Beer Week' specials launched by local breweries, and it was estimated that an additional 2000 people visited Sheffield for the event. In more recent years, the festival has continued to fly the flag for inclusivity, independent spirit and the city's illustrious heritage, firmly establishing itself as one of the most important dates on any beer-lover's calendar.

**sheffieldbeerweek.co.uk**

## Indie Beer Feast

There's really no better way to kick off Sheffield Beer Week than the Indie Beer Feast. Over two days, the old Abbeydale Picture House plays host to some of the country's best brewers, street food vendors and local musicians. From small beginnings on a single day in March 2018, the Indie Beer Feast has grown to encompass two days, four ticketed sessions, and over fifteen hundred attendees. There's also a chance to snap up exclusive brews at the 'Beer of the Festival' competition annually as it challenges those brewers pouring at the event to serve up a new beer via an ever changing theme, from using a seasonal ingredient or taking inspiration from historical beer recipes.

Over the years breweries such as Saint Mars of the Desert, Abbeydale, Thornbridge, North Brewing Co, Sierra Nevada, Cloudwater, Orbit, Wild Card, Neptune, Donzoko, Pastore, Mikkeller and Frau Gruber have all poured at the beer festival. You'll also find pop-up tastings spontaneously held throughout the two days hosted by breweries, cideries and beer writers such as Pete Brown and Adrian Tierney-Jones.

**indiebeerfeast.co.uk**

## CAMRA Steel City Beer

Held in the heart of Kelham Island, an area which consistently manages to be one of Sheffield's most historic and yet happening locations, the CAMRA Steel City & Cider Festival is a post-industrial playground for drinkers of all tastes and inclinations.

Proud to be established and staffed entirely by volunteers, this is an event for the most passionate of beer and cider drinkers.

Taking place in Kelham Island Museum, amongst the treats in store is the Upper Hall, annually transformed by a huge real ale bar. A festival where history comes alive and flows, CAMRA provides not only a commemorative glass for visitors and plenty of brews to sample, but a unique insight into the methods and history of the brewing industry in Sheffield.

## Dronfield Beer & Cider Festival

In one shape or another, the Dronfield Beer & Cider Festival has been serving up suds south of the city every summer since 2013. Building upon the reputation of the much-loved Three Valleys Festival, the independent pubs of Dronfield formed a fringe event to complement the official CAMRA gathering. The result is a smaller festival to check out if you're looking for that pub-crawl feeling.

Organised by the Pioneer Club, with up to fifty real ales and a broad selection of locally brewed ciders on offer, this is another CAMRA festival made by the volunteers. Three days of events for dedicated drinkers, including street food and live performers, kick off with a preview night where you'll take home a commemorative glass and be able to try out the whole beer and cider selection. If you're looking for something outside the city centre to really capture the atmosphere of the real local, why not grab a glass here?

## Thornbridge Peakender

For those who enjoy a taste of the outdoors just as much as the taste of a pint, the Thornbridge Peakender is the perfect weekend away. Taking place in the heart of the Peak District each summer, the three-day festival has built a reputation for bringing together the very best in views and brews that the area has to offer. There's really no better scenery in which to blow away the cobwebs!

Alongside the expected host of eateries, entertainers, and breweries, the element which makes the Peakender such a memorable experience for many is the camping. But whether you choose to spend a night under the stars or simply a day in the sun, there's so many activities to choose from.

Sampling local beers, ciders, and gins might be alright for adults, but if you're looking for more family-oriented fun, there's also options for little ones. It's no surprise that out of all the festivals local to Sheffield, the Peakender is well-known as one to which visitors bring the whole family along.

## Sheffield Food Festival

In a town just as keen on its cuisine as its drink, the Sheffield Food Festival has become the largest free-to-attend event in the city with ease. With a wealth of talent setting up shop in local venues and on the streets every May, as of 2019 the event has been bringing in upwards of 50,000 visitors to Sheffield over its single weekend.

Amongst the many attractions, an Artisanal Market seeks to spotlight food producers and brewers from across the city. Everything from cookery books to craft ales can be explored, providing plenty of tips and treats to take home. The Street Food Market and Eats, Treats, & Beats Festival Village likewise showcase the amazing street food and nightlife on offer in the city each day.

At the centre of the excitement is the Theatre Kitchen, where top local chefs can show you how to get the very best out of Sheffield produce. With so many events to get through, though, it's no wonder many visitors choose to return year after year!

# CONTRIBUTORS

Thanks to all these businesses for being a part of The Sheffield
Beer & Spirits Bible...

| | |
|---|---|
| 60 | ALE CLUB |
| 100 | BEER CENTRAL |
| 66 | BEER DOG |
| 64 | BENCH |
| 66 | BERLIN CALLING |
| 18 | BREW FOUNDATION |
| 22 | CROSSPOOL ALE MAKERS SOCIETY |
| 72 | CUBANA |
| 74 | DEAD DONKEY |
| 102 | DRAM SHOP |
| 24 | EMMANUALES |
| 76 | THE FAT CAT |
| 104 | HOP HIDEOUT |
| 78 | INDUSTRY TAP |
| 28 | KELHAM ISLAND BREWERY |
| 30 | LITTLE CRITTERS BREWING COMPANY |

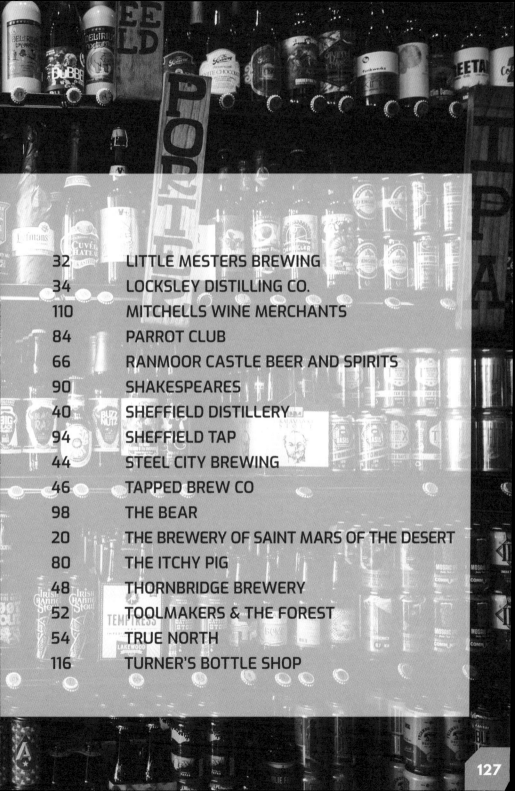

| 32 | LITTLE MESTERS BREWING |
| 34 | LOCKSLEY DISTILLING CO. |
| 110 | MITCHELLS WINE MERCHANTS |
| 84 | PARROT CLUB |
| 66 | RANMOOR CASTLE BEER AND SPIRITS |
| 90 | SHAKESPEARES |
| 40 | SHEFFIELD DISTILLERY |
| 94 | SHEFFIELD TAP |
| 44 | STEEL CITY BREWING |
| 46 | TAPPED BREW CO |
| 98 | THE BEAR |
| 20 | THE BREWERY OF SAINT MARS OF THE DESERT |
| 80 | THE ITCHY PIG |
| 48 | THORNBRIDGE BREWERY |
| 52 | TOOLMAKERS & THE FOREST |
| 54 | TRUE NORTH |
| 116 | TURNER'S BOTTLE SHOP |

**Sheffield Beer & Spirits Bible**
©2021 Meze Publishing Ltd. All rights reserved.
First edition printed in 2021 in the UK.
ISBN: 9781910863886
Thank you to: John Mitchell, Jules Gray, Mike Pomranz, John Wickham & Sean Clarke
Compiled by: Nick Hallam
Written by: Joe Food, Ash Birch, Lizzie Morton & Paul Stimpson
Proofed by: Katie Fisher
Photography by: Marc Barker
Designed by: Paul Stimpson & Phil Turner
Cover art: Jim Connolly (www.jimcportfolio.co.uk)
Printed in Great Britain by Bell and Bain Ltd, Glasgow

Published by Meze Publishing Limited
Unit 1b, 2 Kelham Square
Kelham Riverside
Sheffield S3 8SD
Web: www.mezepublishing.co.uk
Telephone: 0114 275 7709
Email: info@mezepublishing.co.uk